THE HEALING BOX

PAUL REED

Trilogy Christian Publishers
A Wholly Owned Subsidary of Trinity Broadcasting Network
2442 Michelle Drive
Tustin, CA 92780

Cover design by: Colin Kimball

For information, address Trilogy Christian Publishing
Rights Department, 2442 Michelle Drive, Tustin, Ca 92780.
Trilogy Christian Publishing/ TBN and colophon are trademarks of Trinity Broadcasting Network.

For information about special discounts for bulk purchases, please contact Trilogy Christian Publishing.

Manufactured in the United States of America

10 9 8 7 6 5 4 3 2 1

Library of Congress Cataloging-in-Publication Data is available.

ISBN 978-1-63769-028-4 (Print Book)
ISBN 978-1-63769-029-1 (ebook)

Dedicated to:

Pauline Roden Baker

"Well, son, if it were me, I'd get it translated. Maybe there's something inside that could help you change your life for the better, then you could write a book about it."

TABLE OF CONTENTS

The Diary of Second Lieutenant Nguyen Van Nghia

ACKNOWLEDGEMENTS

Special gratitude to Rev. Stephen Kinney, Ralph Gillum, Mike Brown, Dr. Rick Miller, Dr. Toung Ba Van, Dr. Wendell "Fritz" Schautz, Ambassador Luong Thanh Nghi, Ministry of Foreign Relations Hanoi, Nguyen Van Nghia, Vu Thi Gai, Nguyen Van Nghia's immediate family including his grandson Nguyen Thanh Luan and granddaughter Nguyen Thanh Huyen, Ambassador Le Van Bang, Ambassador Le Dzung, Secretary General VNUS Society Bui Van Nghi, Ambassador Nguyen Tam Chien, Huyen Dang, The Dan, Nguyen-the-Suc, Jim Lane, J boy of MLLeddy's, Chapter XIII of 173rd Airborne Brigade Association, David Read, Mike and Gail Lester, Michael Vijil, Manny Mermea, John Doane, Jim Davis, Dale Doucet, Steve Smith, Phil Sturholm, Colin Kimball for the cover design, Communities Foundation of Texas (CFT), and, of course, my son Silas, mom Polly and dad Leo Baker.

Paul Reed

FOREWORD

It is my great honor to write a word of introduction to my friend Paul Reed's book. The word "inspirational" is kicked around a lot these days, perhaps, because, in times of darkness and stress, we are all seeking anything we can find that will inspire us. But I can think of nothing that is so literally and profoundly inspirational as the story of Paul Reed and Nguyen Van Nghia.

It is the tale of two fierce and implacable warriors, each of whom was fighting for honor, for his country, for things he believed in with all his heart. And in this fight, they were pitted against each other, bitterly and violently.

And, for both men, the scars and damage of combat far outlasted the war itself. Paul and Nghia could easily have succumbed to the wounds they sustained, joining their countless slain comrades…but for the unique circumstances, you will read about in *The Healing Box*.

This story has been told in the popular press, in a documentary film, and on TV. But never before by the man who lived it and made it all happen, Paul Reed himself.

Paul is a humble, self-effacing man with no desire for self-aggrandizement. It was with difficulty that his friends managed to persuade him to tell the story from his point of view. But he does so in his own voice, with sometimes blistering honesty and a guileless lack of self-consciousness. I admire his writing a lot.

As the unique friendship that is recounted here grew and matured over the past three decades, Paul is now able to tell Nghia's story as well as his own, putting himself with sympathy and accuracy into the life and head of an enemy combatant—something that would have been unthinkable to Sgt. Paul Reed in 1968, who was then the young soldier launching mortar rounds in the Kontum Highlands of Vietnam against the very man he now writes about with such love.

Can there be anything more profound than a warrior turned peacemaker? It is the story of another Paul on the road to Damascus, the story of the Roman soldier Longinus. It is *this* story of forgiveness and love that arose out of hatred: the story of Paul Reed and the man who became, truly, his comrade-in-arms, Nguyen Van Nghia.

Read on. It will move you as much as it has moved me and everyone else who has been fortunate enough to hear or read it.

Dave Hunsaker
Screenwriter/playwright

WYOMING

A convoy of tractor-trailer trucks rolled toward Kemmerer, Wyoming on old Highway 30, each hauling Washington apples headed for Texas.

I—Paul Reed—in my early thirties, driving the lead truck, am stressed out from days upon days without sleep.

A call came over the radio for "Ridge Runner," my handle on the CB. Jim Thornton, whose handle was "Hard Times," told me not to forget that we were approaching a well-known speed trap and to hold my speed down. I told him, "Don't worry, it's not the time of day for bears to be out; we have to make Texas before tomorrow afternoon."

All three semis came to a stop at the Kemmerer, Wyoming port-of-entry.

I, Hard Times, and the third driver, Dennis Williams, whose handle was "CW," entered the office to have our log books checked and time-stamped. We could see the weigh-station officer was in no hurry, so I headed for the restroom.

Much to my surprise, when I returned, Hard Times and CW were already gone, and another driver from a different trucking company was about to hand his log to the officer.

Realizing my buddies were already on the road and putting distance between us, I cut in front of him and handed my log book to the officer first.

If looks could kill, I would have died right there.

The officer time-stamped my log book, and I headed for the door.

Barely back on the road, and only a few minutes behind my buddies, I could see the other truck leaving the station.

A few miles down the highway, that same truck showed up in my rear-view trying to pass, but there were oncoming cars.

As soon as there were no more, I got over as far as I could, allowing the driver behind me room to see around, but the driver chose not to pass. I grabbed the CB, shouting for the driver to get on around, that I'd not stay there long, but he gave no response.

Within a few moments, the truck was out in the oncoming traffic's lane.

Just one problem.

Headed straight at it, at a high rate of speed, was an oncoming car.

Under normal circumstances, drivers getting passed backed off to help everyone avoid accidents, but not this time. I kept the pedal to the metal, vowing whatever happened, the other driver owned it.

Soon our two trucks were neck and neck and eyeballing each other when the driver in the rig going around shot me his middle finger.

That was injury enough, but things suddenly worsened when drivers of both the truck and the car had to make a decision.

Just as soon as the driver's trailer was inches from the nose of my truck, it swung over, nearly crashing into me. Had I not slammed the brakes, the bar ditch would have been my last option, upside down, wheels in the air.

At last look in the rear-view, that had become the option for the oncoming car, now at rest upside down in a cloud of dust.

The finger, I'd let go but not this. With my temperament, I could not overlook what had just taken place.

There had been radio silence. Until then... I grabbed the mike and screamed for Hard Times and CW if they copied.

Suddenly, that was the driver's wake-up call. Without that call, the unruly driver might have never known that I had company.

Yeah, they got copy. Having learned of my plight, they said they'd be more than happy to help stop the unruly driver for a friendly chat.

All four trucks were in a line only a few feet apart, running at a high rate of speed when the lone driver suddenly slowed to take the nearest exit up ahead. He'd seen the sign pointing toward Salt Lake City.

"See there, Ridge Runner," Hard Times added, actually believing what he was about to say, "You can forget having a discussion with him because he's headed to Salt Lake. Don't forget we gotta be in Texas tomorrow afternoon."

But even though Hard Times and CW dismissed the driver as gone, I stayed angry, vowing to never forget.

The trio decided to stop at Green River and have coffee. Moments later, Hard Times, CW, and I headed back to our trucks. On the way, I countered the other two's assumption they'd never see the lone driver again, saying, "It's not over yet."

All three semis were back rolling.

I got the front door. Following me was Hard Times, and behind him, CW, only a few hundred feet separating one from the other. When the trio rounded a wide right-turning curve, I noticed a lone truck coming from the business district of the town where we had stopped for coffee, about to enter the Interstate heading in our same direction.

When I first noticed the truck, it didn't register who or what the truck might be, but as I approached closer and closer, things were not nearly as blurry as they'd been seconds earlier. It was the driver who narrowly missed sending me to an early grave.

His diversionary plan of exiting toward Salt Lake lulled Hard Times and CW into thinking they'd never see him again, but it hadn't fooled me, and I was about to get even.

Immediately I felt my blood begin to boil. Adrenalin like this wasn't something I'd encountered since combat in Vietnam, but clearly, it was back in charge.

Now back in front, I had to keep the truck I wanted to stop behind me because he had a faster truck.

At exactly the same moment I passed him, I keyed my mike and screamed, "Driver, I got you now! I got you now!"

Over the course of the next ten minutes, CB base stations in the area heard an intense, white-knuckle, adrenaline-pumping, truck driver highway brawl. I kept the driver, who was desperately trying to get around, from passing any way he could as I downshifted to lower gears, making both our trucks go slower and slower.

The lone driver, wanting to get away, only inches from the rear of my trailer, swerved frantically to the right, then the left. To the right, then to the left again and again. Eyeing the swerving truck in the rear view, though, I was adamant about having that conversation CW first proclaimed.

After dropping gear after gear and bringing the rigs to a slower and slower speed, I slammed on the brakes, and all four semi-trucks came to an abrupt stop. I grabbed my double-barrel twelve-gauge I kept stored in my sleeper and dashed toward the rear of my trailer, where the cab of the other truck had barely missed hitting my trailer and came to a stop.

Hard Times had the driver's leg and was prying him out, when I showed up with my shotgun, a cannon loaded with double-ought buck, shouldered and only seconds away from having its trigger pulled.

The driver saw it pointed right at his head, causing his eyes to bug out, but Hard Times, unaware I had approached, never let up and never noticed me with the sawed-off.

That was until he heard my scream for him to get away, "Get out of the way, get out of the way, Hard Times! I'm gonna blow his brains out!"

That's when Hard Times looked up. When he saw me standing there with the double-barrel pointed directly at the driver's head, he let go of the driver's leg and charged me, screaming frantically along the way, "No, no, don't kill him, don't kill him. We'll all go to jail."

Passing cars were curious to see why four trucks were completely stopped and taking up the entire right lane of the Interstate but peeled out when they saw two drivers on the pavement, wrestling over a shotgun, and the wrong end of it pointed toward them.

Seconds after the unruly driver saw Hard Times and me fighting on the pavement, he jobbed his truck in gear and let it rip. It was his chance at getting away. His truck could be seen doing wheel stands, nearly hitting Hard Times and me.

CW, who had refrained from entering the fray, hollered at the two of us still wrestling on the pavement, "He's getting away, ya all."

NORTH VIETNAM

A young Vietnamese boy named Nguyen Van Nghia had been born on August 10, 1928, to a couple who were poor peasants and who died while he was still a boy.

Nguyen Van Nghia had been born and raised in Tay Giang village of Tien Hai district, Thai Binh province, near Haiphong Harbor in the Red River Delta.

In the same small village lived his aunt and uncle, who raised the boy as their own. They would have, perhaps had there been one, taken Nghia to the dentist, but in their village, there was none to be found. Fortunately for young Nghia, he never developed cavities and grew up without ever having a dental exam.

Nghia received food, shelter, and education from his aunt and uncle. He was literate at the young age of four: reading, writing, and math came easy to him.

As he grew on a diet of fish and rice, they instilled in him an appreciation for his fellow man and patriotism. They also taught him to appreciate his culture, making him proud of who he was.

By the time he was a pre-teen, some promising traits were beginning to show, traits like writing, altruism, and humor. Nghia had a sense of humor that most other kids his age did not have.

One day in high school, after returning from lunch at home, he brought a small lizard and put it on the shoulder of one of his classmates while she sat at her desk. She didn't notice it until it had climbed down her blouse, at which time she jumped straight up screaming, hopping, and dancing around the classroom until she could no longer scream, hop and dance. The whole class broke out laughing like it was the funniest thing they'd ever seen. Nghia just sat there grinning from ear to ear.

Of course, the girl was almost in tears; she could feel the lizard moving around under her blouse and really had no idea what the critter was until her jumping made it fall out on the floor and scurry off. By that time, the teacher had figured out who had done it simply by the look on his face: the class jokester, Nghia.

Other times, his uncle took him to the main part of town to meet friends and buy a few things. On the way, they stopped at the local blacksmith shop, his uncle wanting to show Nghia how the pick used in their garden was made. The excursion impressed Nghia greatly.

As he advanced through high school while developing his writing skills, he noticed he liked poetry.

> *I look up at the tall furnace*
> *Welding fire brighter than the stars;*
> *I look up at the tall furnace*
> *And see the blacksmith girl*
> *Looking up at the stars.*
> *Daily she returns home, satchel in hand.*
> *To enjoy a pleasant afternoon,*
> *Still doting on her blacksmith mentor.*
> *See her watch the flowers bloom in the morning*
> *So absorbed in the moment;*
> *She must be scolded by Mom.*
> *Brilliant flames well constantly from the depths of her soul.*

These find the tall furnace,
Stoking the welding fire to be brighter than
the stars
That the blacksmith girl has fixed her eyes on.
She admires the stars as she does the fine
welding line
That she so loves.
Day after day, the girl's hands are busy,
For every tomorrow the furnace yields a
fresh batch of steel.
She feels happy, watching the country grow
stronger,
Flourishing like the morning blooms.
At exam time, the girl is a bouquet of fresh
roses.
The tall furnace makes the future as bright
As the countless stars.

Instead of being doomed to the same life of grinding poverty that they had known, Nghia was given a chance to go to school where he studied both letters (reading and writing) and what was called "the operation," the Vietnamese equivalent of addition, subtraction, multiplication, and division.

It was a very simple school, somewhat similar to the American one-room schoolhouse found in rural areas, but it was enough for a man of his intellect to be noted and for him to eventually excel in his education and develop life skills necessary to support himself and a family.

Nghia was seventeen years old the first time he went into the army—about the time World War II ended. After Nghia's parents died, his brothers lived apart from each other, and he had not yet met his wife. He trained and fought against the French on missions within the northern provinces and

19

received training as a political instructor about the time the American War was beginning.

On one mission during his country's efforts to remove the French from Vietnam, Nghia lost one of his front incisor teeth. As they were all on the side of a hill taking a break, a soldier in front of him fell backward abruptly, hitting a bamboo tube Nghia was drinking from. The edge of the tube hit the tooth, breaking it off, almost causing it to be swallowed.

War terrified Nghia, but he was intensely patriotic. He related to the leaders of the past who fought generation after generation to free their land of foreign domination. He would do his best, knowing it did not matter if he lived or died, so long as he served his country well.

It was 1957 when Nghia finally was able to marry. He worked the land—a peasant faced with the same intense hard work that had led to his parents' early death. But his life was a little better, and he had four children, his first son being born in 1959.

He graduated from the military academy in North Vietnam and was commissioned a second lieutenant assigned to the 304th Division of the People's Army of Vietnam (PAVN), an elite unit assigned some of the most difficult fighting in what became known to the Vietnamese as the American war.

The men of the 304th Division took an oath to serve their country.

Nguyen Van Nghia carried military marching song cards to recite as they marched south down Truong Son mountain range, the link between the north and south, occasionally finding time to write poetry.

Nguyen Van Nghia turned forty years old while fighting the American war in the south.

OFF TO THE ARMY

When I was young, my father assured me that I would be provided the necessary things of life, food, clothing, education, and a roof over my head until I reached the age of eighteen, and longer if I went to college. Additionally, my father informed me, should anything outside of the things he'd mentioned be wanted or desired, it would *not* be paid for by him.

Not long after our conversation, I decided I could make about $20 per month cutting grass. It pleased me to not only have my own money, but it was also rewarding to see the approval on my father's face.

After a few summers of grass cutting, a route manager for the *Dallas Times Herald* offered me an afternoon paper route. "There are about forty customers on the route, and if you have a bicycle, it'll go fast," the manager told me. I delivered papers for about a year on the same bicycle my father had as a kid.

Then, at the corner where a truck dropped bundles of the papers, there were two or three others with bicycles and one with a motorcycle. A Honda. Not long after starting my new route, the boy with the motorcycle said he'd be glad to help me throw my papers if I, in turn, helped him throw his. Pointing to his motor, he said, "Both routes could be thrown in about the same time as one—with this."

Nine months later, the prospect of having my own motorcycle came up, but I was only thirteen. "Don't forget," my father told me, "I'm providing the necessary things, and a motorcycle is not one of them."

A year later, only days away from my fourteenth birthday, I took delivery of a brand new nifty-thrifty Honda 50. My dad had come around and agreed to pay for half if I had managed to save half of the $275 cost, which I somehow did.

Now, with my own motorcycle, I managed to find others in my school who had motorcycles too, such as the Messina brothers three streets over.

One sunny afternoon, the three of us, each with his own motorcycle, approached a footbridge that crossed a creek near our houses. The twins watched while I gunned my motor and began crossing the bridge. Actually, the small bridge was meant only for foot traffic, so it was no surprise I wound up in the creek bed below, knocked smooth out.

As I lay submerged in the creek bed below, water flowing over me, I came back to consciousness with one of the twins on each side frantically screaming for me to wake up. When I finally did, I couldn't make out what happened: I was foggy-headed like when first waking in the morning. But a large gaping hole over my right eye, caused by hitting a sharp rock in the creek bed, was bleeding profusely, and the brothers knew I needed help. They got me on the buddy seat behind one of their motors and took off while I held my head in both hands.

Within minutes, I stood—wobbled—on my doorstep, waiting for my mother to come to the front door, a half-inch open wound on my cheek bleeding all over me like nothing the twins had ever seen.

When Polly, my mother, answered the doorbell, her face was wrought with fear when she saw my shirt covered in blood and me about to fall.

Three different motorcycles and three serious wrecks later, my next-door neighbor named Brendan came home on leave from Germany. A year earlier, he had joined the army and became a paratrooper, and had gotten stationed overseas. I stared at his photos, wondering what jumping from planes would be like as the young man tried explaining.

"Could it be worse than several motorcycle wrecks and smashing into rocks at the bottom of creek beds?" I asked the young paratrooper.

There were several acres of open land in the back of the elementary school, which I attended through the sixth grade, where some older boys introduced what came to be known as parasailing.

Linked to the rear bumper of a pickup truck was about a hundred-foot rope that was attached to an old World War II surplus parachute. Anyone who was a risk-taker and adventurous enough got a ride, and when someone said, "Who's next?" I raised my hand. For a few moments after harnessing up, nothing happened, but that all changed when the pickup began moving forward, slowly at first.

Then, the person in the harness that was attached to the rope tied to the truck had to chase after the truck until the chute they were strapped in inflated and began lifting them toward the sky. The chasing usually didn't last long, and as long as the truck kept moving, the person being towed floated above the earth on the most joyous ride of their life. However, that would change after only a few minutes.

Just when they got comfortable floating around the open field, the pickup driver would slam on his brakes, bringing the truck to a screeching halt. That was when everyone freaked out, realizing one was on his own without knowing what to do next. Yet, when I hit the ground, I felt energized. I'd found a new pastime and understood exactly what my neighbor friend, the paratrooper, had said.

Extracurricular activities interested me more than high school. I never stopped to realize the importance of education but never fully understood what education was all about or that it was the groundwork for my entire life. That attitude led me to sign up for a course that got me out of class at noon: Distributive Education. The course's only requirement, other than passing grades, was that I would work a certain amount of hours at a job. I was good with that.

One day in high school, I told the school counselor I wanted to learn Spanish. She told me that it was a fabulous goal and went for my records. When she returned, she said, "It is an honorable thing, learning a new language, but..." she hesitated, "you have to pass English first."

John F. Kennedy inspired a lot of Americans with his speech about civic action and public service. "Ask not what your country can do for you but what you can do for your country," he said. At the time, I failed to recognize its full meaning, but the older I got, the more I saw it as motivation.

A year later, I approached my father. I wanted to join the army. I wanted to be a paratrooper like Brendan, the guy next door. I was experienced with a parachute, the wind hitting me in the face, had heard what the army was like from a garrison soldier, I'd heard JFK's speech. If there ever was a feeling of duty, honor, and country, I told my dad, I felt it now. I'd watched the *Nightly News* several times. I'd witnessed scenes of soldiers fighting in a jungle far from home. Yet, I never let on to dad what my intentions were—becoming a soldier and fighting in a faraway war.

At seventeen, I was ready to join and be the man I'd been born to be. Besides, I wasn't all that good at school, and if my father saw it my way, there were other opportunities I believed I could master, I said to my dad.

My father pretended to read a book while I talked, but he was actually listening while hoping it was just a bad dream. He had high hopes for me. He wanted me to be a professional man like himself, graduate college, make something of myself, have his grandkids.

When I slipped and said something about fighting, he realized he was not dreaming. He laid the book he was reading on his lap and looked me squarely in the eye, saying, "What exactly is it you need from me?"

"A signature," I said, "you need to sign for me because I'm only seventeen." My expectations fell flat after he began objecting. At first, I believed dad would come around; then, as he continued talking, I heard him say flat out he'd not sign.

He told me, his only son, he'd rather prefer I got my high school diploma first. "After that, you will be eighteen, and you can do as you please."

I straddled my motorcycle, facing steps leading upward to my high school, revving the engine. Suddenly I popped the clutch and climbed the steps, both amusing and amazing the students hoping to get to class on time by speeding down the hall at full-throttle, jamming gears like a jockey on a race track. I was full of exuberance, laughing—having the laugh of my life the full length of the hall. My fun ended when I almost ran over the principal, who waited for me outside, at the end of the hall.

When I arrived home early, my mom asked why I was home not at the regular time. I'd gotten expelled for three days. "Three days," she said, "that means you'll miss finals. If you don't take those exams, you'll be back next year."

She got me in the car, and once inside the school, she marched me to the principal's office, where she demanded her son be allowed to take his finals. When the principal resisted, she reminded him that if I were not allowed to take the finals, I would be back again next year.

Horrified by the thought of a returning hellion, the principal agreed to let me take my finals. My geography teacher had borne the task of passing me, though my grades were failing. Mr. Godfrey, the teacher, set me in a corner, not facing the class, and informed me I'd have to write an essay. The essay was to be on everything I knew about an automobile between its front and rear bumpers. The paper garnered me an A, raising failing grades to a passing D, and I got my diploma that summer.

When I walked into the army recruiting office, there was nothing but a smile on my face. My thoughts were only of the fun I'd have jumping out of planes and floating back to earth, like parasailing. The idea that I would get paid to jump from planes overshadowed any other thoughts. There were never any thoughts of getting killed, maimed for life, or even dying.

The recruiter, Staff Sergeant (E-6) Russell, fit my youthful image of what a paratrooper should be. Well over six feet tall, lean, hard, and broad-shouldered, he looked the well-trained professional in his regulation crew cut and khaki uniform. He also knew the right things to say to convince any young man to join.

Army Airborne was a special life for a few like me. The training was rigorous, too tough for many boys my age, he mentioned. But Sgt. Russell observed me carefully, as though sizing me up. Then he would say he thought I might have what it took to make it in such an elite force. The combination of subtle challenge and reinforcement of my fantasies was just the right touch needed to win over a new enlistee.

I signed the paperwork without leaving the office to think about what I would be doing for the next three years of my life. I agreed to take twenty-four hours to get packed, then to ship out the next day, following the successful completion of a physical exam, a formality.

I hollered "present!" when my name was called, then boarded the bus taking me to basic training at Fort Polk, Louisiana.

THAI BINH, NORTH VIETNAM

A military vehicle sped through villages in the Thai Binh province, broadcasting urgent messages.

"Troops are needed. We must run the American invaders out and reunify the country."

The country had been at peace since the end of the French occupation, but the loudspeakers told of a new occupation, that of the Americans. From their dinner tables, villagers heard Hanoi's call to duty. Anyone within earshot understood exactly what it meant: the country was at war, the messages gave rise to a sense of patriotism.

Thai Binh, a province located approximately seventy miles southeast of Hanoi, was a logical place to broadcast that message. Living there were more military personnel of eligible age than anywhere in North Vietnam.

Nguyen Van Nghia, Viet Minh veteran of the French War, decided to fight again when he heard the appeal. A peaceful and respected family man, who fellow villagers looked upon as an uncle figure.

His country had been occupied far too long, he told himself, and there was much discord. They successfully drove the French from his country, and now they would have to kick out the Americans.

Nghia, already a veteran, a survivor of one war, answered his nation's call to fight in another.

Now, after four months of walking the Ho Chi Minh Trail (Truong Son mountain range), the proud People's Army Vietnam (PAVN) soldier and his unit had reached their destination in the south. The trails they traveled through Laos led them back inside Vietnam by crossing the Da Krong River.

Not far into the southern province, there were steep mountains, covered with tall hardwoods towering over thirty meters forty-eight centimeters (hundred feet), having branches and leaves so tightly packed not a ray of sunshine got through.

Their maps indicated they were in the northwestern part of Kontum Province, near the tri-border intersections of Laos, Cambodia, and Vietnam.

But getting there was no easy task: there were no trains, buses, or ships taking them; they had to walk carrying heavy backpacks and huge loads using both hands all day long.

The unit experienced death, dysentery, and deserters, who got eaten by tigers as they ran. Those who didn't run knew the identities of those who did, tearfully listened to their screams as they were eaten alive. Remains of what the tigers left were buried somewhere along the trail in unmarked graves, only to melt into the jungle floor.

Never enough food, water, medicine, or medical care, never a spare moment in a twenty-four-hour day. It could be said that along the 800–900 km journey, the North Vietnamese army unit encountered nothing peaceful.

Everything became a threat: the enemy in the air, the enemy on the ground who watched them traverse the trails, hunger, tigers, chemical defoliants, poisonous snakes, leeches, malaria-carrying mosquitoes, treacherous elevations, horrendous heat, torrential rains, burdensome weight, and lack, among many other things, of sufficient footwear.

Many started their long trek southward, wearing sandals made from old tires strapped to their feet with strips of inner tubes…then decided to go barefoot as sharp rocks hurt their feet less.

A position for a bunker system was needed; the unit traveled there to assist other units from North Vietnam in their conquest of the reunification of the north and south.

Their commander studied their maps. He finally picked a natural, well-concealed area of high ground that would give their unit an advantage over any other.

Their main purpose in the south—ambushes.

Their location, according to old French maps, indicated they were on a hill showing an elevation of 1,064 meters or over 3,000 feet high, overlooking a huge valley facing west. "A perfect location," Nghia said to the company commander before going off to assist the different platoons at digging in and building bunkers. Great attention was given to the placement of each bunker by Nghia, while other officers determined what action and how best to implement a plan should they need to abandon their current position. They named their location Cherry Hill in honor of large numbers of fellow countrymen whose blood was shed not far away.

A reconnaissance team was organized.

Nghia and other team members were sent to locate a site that could be used in case of emergency, that is, if the unit had to escape being overrun by the Americans or destroyed by their heavy artillery.

When the team returned, they reported their find to the commander. "An excellent site," Nghia said, pointing it out on the map, "only a little over two hundred meters from here. It's wedged deeply between two mountains. Thickly covered with trees. And we know you'll like this, commander: there's a cool mountain stream flowing from one side to the other."

"That's good, but does the site provide cover from the air?" the commander wanted to know.

"Yes, sir. The site is wedged between two mountains, and with dense foliage encasing it, there's no way for even the sun to get through. High overhead trees block not only sunlight but also smoke from our cooking fires. The location provides natural concealment from the air and from ground troops too."

"Good," the commander said. "We will use it as our diversionary camp. If the Americans come too close, we will fool them into thinking we have vacated where we are now, but in actuality, we will have moved over there and lived to fight again."

The commander understood since the Americans had superior air power and artillery, they had to avoid all combat until they had the advantage. "Until then," he told his men, "we will avoid losing as many men as possible. In this war, we must outthink and outmaneuver the enemy."

Then the commander turned to Nghia with detailed expectations.

He said, "Lieutenant Nghia, your team members will lead the entire company there. I want the men from all platoons to learn the trail, going and coming, like the back of their hand. Once your team arrives, have the team leader instruct them how to hang their hammocks and make separate areas for cooking, ammo storage, and medical supplies. Let everyone familiarize themselves with where everything is stored. I expect everything to be according to full military discipline, neat and orderly." Nghia and his men were taking it all in, nodding up and down that they understood when he continued, "When you're finished, lead the men back here for further instructions, is that clear?"

"Yes, sir," they said, and as they raised their hands to salute, he said he required one more thing.

"You are to use a stopwatch, and let's see how long a round trip there and back takes. It's imperative we know how long evacuation takes should the enemy's artillery hit, or even worse, they penetrate this position with their infantry. Is that clear?"

"Yes, sir," the men said as they saluted, and before returning their salute, the commander told the men to join the others and eat some rice and *Nuoc mam*.

Once the men had eaten, the commander requested each soldier report to him, and they were to gather around and listen.

He told the men, while holding a newspaper at out-stretched arms so all could see, that he'd gotten it from his political officer. "Inside, conveyed with a great deal of senti-ment, is a letter of encouragement from President Ho Chi Minh to lawyer Nguyen Huu Tho I'd like to read you. This letter will make you proud you are in this battle to save our country and make two Vietnams into one, again. Hearing this from our beloved leader will remind you of why you fight, why you are away from your families, and why you sacrifice." Then after a brief pause and staring intently into each of their eyes, he began reading Ho Chi Minh's letter.

> Dear Mr. Lawyer Nguyen Huu Tho, the chairman and many high-ranking men in the South Vietnam liberation group and soldiers,
>
> While our soldiers and civilians of two regions are continuously collecting many, many victories against Americans to get our freedom, the liberation of South Vietnam declared in large num-bers to fight the American and South

Vietnamese soldiers to the last drop of blood.

We have had seven years of guidance from our clever southern liberation leaders and hero soldiers. We fought together bravely and destroyed many plans of the enemy; we have killed more than a million Americans and their allies. The Americans have been crushed and destroyed everywhere. With the momentum of our victories, the soldiers and people of South Vietnam rose up and attacked everywhere.

They fought in high spirit and created so much confusion for the army of South Vietnam.

Our ancestors and people are proud of our heroes.

Because the Americans were crushed in many battles, they went crazy and started battles everywhere. They flew and bombed North Vietnam. The Americans have a big mouth and lie. They say they want a cease-fire and peace but continue shelling and bombing, but that won't stop our people from fighting. The lying won't stop our people. We will fight until our enemies leave our land. Together we're strong and will survive.

Our goals and our strategy is to fight the Americans and liberate South Vietnam. We work and fight together with the liberation army in our country and also outside our country with many of our friends and allies of the world and even anti-war American supporters.

We will beat strong and evil America. We will beat them with our high spirit fighting and united people— our soldiers and people of the south liberation group are together and brave. We keep up our high spirit with millions of people of South Vietnam.

We will succeed and bring peace for the entire country from north to south.

We will not stop fighting the Americans. Seventeen million people of the north will support the fighting and produce our sources for our brothers and sisters in the south.

Together we are strong and sure of victory.

One day our entire country will be united.

North and south together we celebrate.

I am taking this time to get my thoughts to our seniors and soldiers, soldiers' mothers, and all brave south liberation people and kids. A big hug and kiss.

Finally, to our chairman and south liberation leaders after the victory.

Hanoi 6/9/1967
Ho Chi Minh

KIAS

It was Jeffrey Ratzlaff, a friend of mine from the United States, who gave me my first glimpse of Vietnam. The man had been there for about six months. His uniform appeared old, torn, soiled like it had never been washed. Boots, no longer black, looked like brown rough-out leather, with huge cracks between their upper and lower parts.

Dark circles under his eyes revealed he needed rest and had no proper nutrition. He had aged well past his years. Yet Ratzlaff was considered healthy compared to a second man I met that day.

The man was drawn to the silver wings on my uniform. As he approached, a unit patch on the stranger's uniform indicated he'd served with the 173rd Airborne Brigade. He wanted to know to which unit the newbie paratrooper in the starched khaki uniform with bloused jump boots had been assigned. When he heard "the 173rd," he froze. Then the man's eyes seemed to focus on some faraway place as they widened in horror.

Now standing face-to-face only inches apart, it appeared the man was about to turn violent when what he said next hit me with a one-two punch, "I just hope you like killin', boy."

Obviously, I could see the man had a short fuse, but I answered softly, "Oh yeah? Why's that?" And then, with a twisted demeanor, the man spewed out, "Cuz you'll get to do plenty where you're headed."

In the Central Highlands area of Pleiku, I located my battalion's HHQ (higher headquarters) tent. The XO (executive officer) assigned me to Alpha Company of the First Battalion 503rd Parachute Infantry Regiment, one of the 173rd's four Infantry battalions.

My company was in Kontum, the XO said while stepping outside to show me the direction of the airstrip. "Get yourself over there as soon as possible," pointing toward a perforated steel plate runway not far off. "And when a Caribou with the tail number of A-374 lands, you get aboard and make sure you don't miss your flight."

Once I stepped off the plane and onto what I believed was landing strip no. 1 in Kontum, the pilots wasted no time in getting back in the air.

I stood there a moment, watching the plane leave. There were no horns honking, no sounds of kids playing in the distance, and no ice cream trucks in the neighborhood.

I was alone.

In all of my nineteen years, I'd never been as alone.

Alpha Company had gotten the word. They were to rendezvous with me at the airstrip, and they waited nearby.

*Alpha Company, First Battalion 503rd Parachute Infantry
Regiment, February 1968. Captain Davis, back row, far left.*

After linking up with Alpha Company, we moved a few
clicks (or kilometers, in military talk) to an obscure outpost
named Poli Klang.

The Special Forces camp was one of twenty-six that were
situated about a click east of the Laotian and Cambodian bor-
ders and strung out many miles along the Vietnamese border,
running north and south. The one I had just walked into was
one of two in Kontum Province. It was perched upon slightly
higher ground than Laos and Cambodia and provided a full
view of the Ho Chi Minh Trail less than a click away.

Indigenous personnel, who often fought alongside
Americans, killed a wild hog. The idea was to treat the
Americans visiting the camp to some hospitality, a home-
cooked meal. I watched a man slice a hog into many pieces,
then look up and smile toward me as if to say this was going
to be good. After forcing a smile and nodding up and down

like I approved, I went back to my platoon, opting for canned C-rations instead.

The next day I was facing west toward the Ho Chi Minh trail when I heard what I thought was thunder, meaning rain was about to happen. However, there were no clouds, and the sky was unusually clear, but I was clueless about what made the sounds. Suddenly at eye level, in the direction of the trail, I noticed a row of clouds that looked like dust clouds behind a pickup truck on a dirt road. These were not white clouds; these were dirty, earthly-looking clouds that billowed upward toward the sky and rolled at a high rate of speed.

North Vietnamese troops hurrying along on the trail never heard the B-52s flying miles overhead, but when their bombs detonated, the ground underneath me vibrated, and I could feel it over a click away. The seven hundred and fifty-pound bombs, when detonating, sounded identical to thunder. It was my first introduction to what became known as Rolling Thunder. I didn't have to be closer than I was to know entire units carrying supplies and ammunition to the south were getting pulverized, decimated, annihilated.

Not more than two days at Poli Klang, company platoon leaders were dispatched by Captain Jim Davis to the command post. There they were given details of a new search-and-destroy mission.

Davis's briefing outlined information that PAVN troops had built a bunker complex on one of the ridges towering high above the valley. Coordinates identifying its exact location on the map showed the elevation to be 1064 meters.

That afternoon, Alpha Company loaded helicopters for a heliborne combat assault. Someone said they hoped the LZ would be cold, a term I heard once I got to Vietnam but didn't really understand yet.

Choppers dropped almost a hundred of us five to six hundred meters west of the identified enemy bunker complex. Late that afternoon, after spending time searching the area of operation, Capt. Davis noticed a perfect spot for a night defensive perimeter and had us dig fox holes, forming a circle or "perimeter" in military vernacular, about ten to fifteen meters apart.

That afternoon, I scribbled a letter to my folks:

> 17/March/68
> Sunday Aft.
>
> Hi Mom and Dad,
>
> ...We are on a big mountain north of Pleiku about thirty-five or forty-five miles, getting ready to go up the next mountain beside it, which is about twice as high, except for one problem, there are PAVN at the top, in bunkers waiting for us. For three days now, we have poured artillery, napalms plus 750 lb. bombs, mortars, everything, and a few of them are still there. See, if you're dug in about six feet underground, the only thing that will bounce you out is a B-52 bomb raid. B-52s mean death...
>
> —Excerpt of a letter I
> wrote to my parents

41

After the sunset, my platoon zeroed in our eighty-one-millimeter mortar, firing several rounds in the opposite direction of the hill we had orders to assault.

The next morning, Alpha Company advanced toward the summit of Hill 1064 in a column that looked like a string of aunts moving up a huge mountain. About the time the point platoon could be seen through the dense vegetation, the enemy opened up with AKs killing both James G. Blackshear and Patrick J. Tremblay with bullets right between their eyes.

James G. Blackshear

Patrick J. Tremblay

Moments later, mortar rounds from the enemy location began whizzing towards us. The instant I heard their mortar tube spit one round, I saw everyone shuck their backpacks and hit the ground. I did the same. I didn't get scared until I heard fellow grunts cry out to their momma, their families, even to God. At that point, I knew and understood we were in a bind, and things could only get worse.

Captain Davis radioed ahead to the point platoon for a sitrep (situation report).

He got word of two KIAs (those killed in action).

"Don't leave them behind," Davis said while considering pulling the men back at a safe distance. "Do not let them lay. And don't get any more killed in the process," he added.

It was an exercise in futility. Because of intense enemy fire, both Blackshear and Tremblay laid where they fell. Enemy fire made retrieving their bodies impossible.

PAVN snipers were firing from an elaborate fortress sitting atop the main ridgeline facing west, which we identified as Hill 1064. The slopes leading up to the bunkers were laced with trenches circling the summit of the hill, all connected and spiraling downward among large trees. They had natural protection from artillery, air, and napalm strikes because of the tall, tightly packed, triple canopy trees overhead. The vegetation encircling them rendered them nearly invisible from both air and to Alpha Company.

Any unit, regardless of which army, would have a long uphill struggle and be exhausted when they reached the peak of the summit. Besides the exhaustion of getting to the top of the hill, not to mention horrendous heat and humidity, PAVN snipers had a clear view of the valley below and could take out almost anyone.

Sounds of enemy mortars blasting off were fear enough, but the guessing game of knowing where they'd explode, ripping flesh to shreds in seconds after their fifteen to twenty-second in-air-flight gave anyone the shakes.

"I hate that sound," the guy lying next to me said; we were ready to make a run for the top of the hill and kill the enemy when one exploded about fifteen meters to our front, making both of us rethink moving in any direction.

Alpha Company had already lost two men. After learning the enemy's fire had everyone pinned down and that snipers were dead set on keeping them from retrieving their dead, Davis gave the order to pull back and establish a night defensive perimeter not far down the hill toward the valley.

Me, humping the eighty-one-millimeter mortar tube to our new perimeter during the Battle for Hill 1064. March 1968.

Once the company hustled, at a dead heat, over to a new mountaintop and finished digging foxholes, we realized we were surrounded. The revelation of that came by a sniper firing a single round; things escalated quickly after that as we began returning fire. Moments before the massive fire-fight intensified, a man had taken a round and flip-flopped on the ground like a fish out of water beside a huge rock.

The enemy sniper's round penetrated the man's chest and exited through his back, ripping two bullet holes, one in the front and one in the back. Disabling him to breathe through his nose or mouth, the air traveled through the two freshly made bullet holes. His wound was called a sucking chest wound, and, besides needing surgery immediately, it made normal breathing impossible.

The sun baked us with temperatures over a hundred, but that didn't stop the enemy, whose goal was killing us all. Inbound automatic weapons, poorly aimed RPGs (rocket-propelled grenades) ripping treetops, and ChiCom grenades flying at us all proved they were dead set on making their goal a reality.

But Capt. Davis and his men were not about to let that happen.

With the realization that we were in the fight of our lives, every weapon we had spewed blazing hot lead toward the enemy, who stayed hidden behind huge rocks and heavy green foliage while a medic did everything possible to save the young sergeant's life.

Davis got battalion on the horn (radio), screaming above the raging firefight that he needed a dust-off, and he needed it right now.

While the inbound chopper was yet feathering down, enemy bullets hit one of the pilots in the foot and thwarted their landing. Enemy firing forced the bird to be waived-off three additional times, but the pilots kept flying against orders to return to base. Even after getting hit, they made every attempt at getting the wounded man to much-needed surgery.

I tried to comfort Daniel Burr as he lay groaning on the ground, bullets whizzing overhead, but he didn't want the comfort I had, low crawled over, to offer. Instead, he was getting out of this hellhole, he said, and me and everyone else staying behind were the unlucky ones, but he was happy he got the million-dollar wound and was getting out and going home, adding, "Don't feel sorry for me."

I watched his condition worsen second by second, but he never realized the seriousness because his body was in shock. Then Davis got word to the grunts holding the enemy off on the east side of the perimeter of his plan to use firepower like never before, massive, non-stop, with no letup between bursts so that the chopper could land, and it worked. Suddenly Michael Vejil, Scott Smith, Jerry Thomas, myself, and one or two others hustled Burr on the bird, and he was gone.

I was happy for him. He was getting out of the hellhole, but that happiness only lasted a few minutes. A few moments later, Davis got a call on the radio. Burr had expired.

Daniel was thinking he was going home. It just wasn't the home he was thinking of.

Sgt. Daniel L. Burr, died during the Battle of Hill 1064: March 17th, 1968. Alpha Company 1/503d 173rd Airborne.

Our perimeter was probed from several directions but never penetrated. One enemy we could see that was killed just outside our perimeter by a claymore mine was drug away, but we didn't know how many more, and no one dared leave to go to count. Thousands of rounds were exchanged, and we fought our hearts out, content to never give up, but the thought of everyone not making it could be seen on everyone's face.

Suddenly Davis announced a fire mission for the eighty-one-millimeter crew. As we prepared mortar rounds that would pulverize the enemy, Davis announced the enemy over on Hill 1064 were in for a big surprise—he told the FDC (Fire Direction Center) to put rounds directly on top of the enemy.

I grabbed a round and poked it halfway in the tube while gunner John Burkhart adjusted the gunsight, and FDC Norman Belmore checked the coordinates one last time.

I said to Davis, "Round hangin', sir," and all that stood between that instant in time and killing enemy was one word. I waited…

Fire!

I released the round, and it exited the tube with an ear-piercing *boom* echoing throughout the valley.

Davis was in the pit. He'd given me the command to fire, and he heard the round exit the tube. Still, Burkhart announced, "Round on the way, sir."

Davis, watching the round leave the tube through field glasses, saw it explode about twenty-five meters shy of its intended target.

"Add twenty-five meters," he said to the FDC.

I hung another round.

I (assistant gunner), hanging an eighty-one-millimeter mortar round, about to fire during the Battle for Hill 1064. March 1968. John Burkhart (gunner), in the pit holding his ears, lower center.

Suddenly I heard *"fire!"* and let the round go.

This time success. *Wham!* It exploded exactly where Davis wanted. Squarely in the middle of enemy bunkers on the summit of 1064.

"Quickly, quickly," Davis wanted more "death from above" in the exact place.

FDC frantically called out, "Twelve rounds. Charge four. Fire for effect. Fire at will."

Before hearing the first rounds explode, I had launched dozens of eighty-one-millimeter high explosive mortar rounds whizzing toward the enemy.

It doesn't happen but maybe in one out of a thousand— the eighty-one-millimeter mortar team and I got lucky. One of the rounds I'd sent streaming toward the enemy hit and exploded directly inside their ammunition storage area, causing another explosion, larger than what a single round could make. It's called "a secondary."

This was the hope of any mortar crew because it would kill anyone nearby and reduce the enemy's amount of ammo and their ability to fire back. Fifteen more eighty-one-millimeters were fired before Davis halted the mission.

The next morning, as the sun was about to rise, Alpha Company prepared for its final assault on Hill 1064. Every weapon we had was checked for functionality, magazines checked for ammo, grenades, and knives readied for combat. There was no chatter to be heard as the men realized this might be our last day to live.

About halfway up the summit, there was mild resistance: AKs, SKSs, and an RPG…but none unlike the day before. Still, Davis was in no mood for more casualties.

Floating in the South China Sea was an aircraft carrier.

"Gimme that handset," Alpha Company commander said to his radio telephone operator, Wendell "Fritz" Schautz.

For a few seconds, Davis fumbled with his list of pushes (frequencies) and got frustrated by the increasing sound of movement and chatter atop the hill.

Suddenly, Fritz, who was lying beside him in the prone position, had managed to get a Navy FDC center on the horn before Davis knew what had come down.

He didn't want to strafe, Davis screamed through the handset. He didn't want mini-guns either. Then, louder, sharper, and more direct, he called out the coordinates as clear as possible and said he wanted napalm. After repeating what the FDC thought they'd heard, he was told they'd be on their way in a few seconds.

In only a few minutes, two Navy jets screamed overhead, packing two oblong tanks of thick gasoline-laden jelly underneath their wings.

As the forward air controller circled overhead, the pilot radioed Davis to pop smoke. Seconds later, green smoke floated upward, marking Alpha Company's forward position.

To our front, all ninety or hundred men of Alpha Company had spread wide on the steep slope pointed to the top of Hill 1064. Everyone hugged the only thing that gave them comfort—the ground—but even it trembled.

After circling once or twice, the first jet came in at tree-top level and let go of two cigar-looking canisters that plummeted end over end toward the enemy, hitting a little shy of the target. In the distance, another lined up and directly above the Alpha Company troops, dropped two canisters making it a one-two punch on the hilltop.

Everything to their front was on fire.

No longer could they hear sounds of chatter coming from the top of the summit and no AKs, RPGs, or grenades. We had a clear path and no casualties. Once inside the enemy's position, we discovered shallow graves and enemy dead in every direction.

Before breaching the hill, Alpha Company recovered both KIAs who'd earlier taken bullets. They were lying face down, burned, and swollen beyond recognition.

The grunts often received letters from friends and relatives back home who wrote soldiers hopefully to help them pass the time until they got home. I got regular letters from the grandmother of one of the guys I was about to stuff in a body bag, and it made my insides ache. Later she wrote that she'd gotten word he'd been killed but never knew how or any of the gory details, and I vowed she would never learn.

When we, grunts, rolled them over, we were sickened by what we saw.

Their eye sockets were void of eyeballs, they'd been eaten by maggots, and maggots were still rolling around inside where the eyeballs used to be.

The visual was enough to make anyone throw up, but it got worse.

When we tried hoisting the rotting bodies by their arms, the bodies were going in unzipped body bags, the burned flesh slipped off their bones like overcooked chicken.

Then it happened.

I vomited.

THE POET

One afternoon the PAVN commander came above ground to inspect the bunker complex they'd built overlooking the valley facing west. His office entrance consisted of a hole leading down in the earth that had been dug as close and parallel to the tree trunk that diggers could get it, and in between at least two of the four roots that protruded outwardly from the tree trunk. The towering roots, reaching at least twenty meters vertically on the tree trunk, enabled the tall tree to stand steady at great heights.

As he pulled himself upward and out the small entrance, he took note of Lt. Nguyen Van Nghia, the soldier from Thai Binh, flipping pages in a little book nearby. Ordinarily, that would not garner the attention of a commander, but in this case, the soldier's frustration level was beginning to show, and it made the commander curious, so he decided to have a look.

When Nghia saw his commander approaching, he quickly jumped to his feet.

"You can stand at ease," the commander said while returning the salute. "You know," he said, "I couldn't help but notice the intense attention you are paying to that little book in your hands," pointing to it with his index finger.

The commander, from the north himself, knew it was customary for men to keep diaries and that topics generally alluded to things concurrent with their personalities.

Possessing that knowledge only made him curious as to what one of his soldiers wrote, so he asked.

"No, sir," Nghia replied, "I'm not writing anything about the military," stopping himself short of a full explanation. "Well, not too much anyway, only sometimes. Mostly I write things about my wife, my family and, the life and love we all had before the war. Actually, I was searching for that exact poem but can't remember the page."

"Mostly poetry?" the commander asked.

"Yes, sir."

Before the commander had a chance to further ask anything, Nghia spoke up and mentioned his plan was to read it frequently in the hope of not growing lonely.

"You are right," came the reply, "to ward off boredom, we will all need something to remind us of our families and home. Do you mind if I see it up close?"

"Not at all," Nghia said as he handed the book to his commander.

Its pages had been sown together. The outer cover appeared to be alligator skin, different from others he'd seen, and by flipping its pages, he could see inside it had rag instead of rice paper. After a moment of admiring before giving it back, he said he didn't remember seeing one like it before.

"I'm proud of it," Nghia said, noting others typically had "plain covers, plain rice paper, and glue binding, but this one with hand stitching is special. Would you like to hear how the little book came to me, sir?"

"I'd like that very much," the commander said.

"Well, in Tai Giang village of Tien Hai district where I'm from, my wife bought it off the shelf in a store near our house." Nghia paused to gather his thoughts. When he continued, he said, "We heard the loudspeakers call for troops to go south. Naturally, as a family man, my wife and I had long discussions about my going back in the army and fighting the Americans and how it might affect the family, but she said the nation needed me and I must go.

"Since I was newly commissioned as a second lieutenant in the army, she hosted a going-away dinner. As we sat beside the table, she put my hands in hers and told me something I'll never forget saying, 'Husband, your job as a soldier will be very dangerous and will have many hardships, but there is a way your wife can always be with you.'"

"Is that right?" the commander said, scrutinizing what Nghia said very carefully as he handed the book back.

"Yes sir, well, she knew I liked to write poetry and told me that when she handed this to me," said Nghia, holding the book with both hands while looking the commander in the eyes, "She said, 'When you fill its pages with poems and poetry about your wife, you can have me by your side each time you read them.'

"So, commander, sir, that's what I have done. As we traveled the Truong Son mountain range, its pages got filled with poems and memories of her, my family, and our country. She told me she believes both of us will return to her."

"Both of you?"

"Yes," Nghia explained, "She said she had a dream: both I and the little book will come back to her. That belief principle was handed down to her from her ancestors."

The commander, reflecting on his personal ancestry, said, "What do *you* believe?"

"Sir, we lost many thousands of men only a short distance from here in Dak To. From that battle just a few months ago, we know the Americans are very brutal. We have all heard how they will kill us and cut out our livers and hearts and eat them. They are barbarians. Surviving will be difficult, if not impossible, and not only that, we are here for the war's duration.

"Based upon what happened at Dak To, it's possible we are in the path of destruction, and no one will survive." He continued, "If not death from the Americans, many will die of starvation, disease, snake bites, or malnutrition. Food supplies are essentially non-existent. Our only hope to eat, other than tree roots, is scavenging can food the Americans leave behind in their fox holes."

"Will I survive," he asked the commander, "Will both of us return to her? Ahhhh, if only I myself could believe. But, if I can have her by my side when my time to die comes, I will not be alone—that is most important!"

"That's all very interesting," the commander said. He understood war, the horrors of it, and while not wanting to cast doubts as a pessimist on what he'd just heard, he said nothing but privately doubted the man's wife had told him correctly. "Did you compose the poems yourself?" the commander probed.

"No, not all, but the ones of my wife, my country and family, those I wrote. Some speak to me about why I am a People's Army soldier in the first place. Others why this fight is so important to win and others why we never give up during our difficult times."

"And for her," the commander asked, "did you reciprocate? Did you also give her a gift from you?"

"Certainly," he answered, "I am a veteran of the French war and have lived long enough to learn proper etiquette. For her, as a remembrance of me, I fashioned a flute from a short piece of bamboo. I told her when she played to listen to the melody, and she would have me by her side too. She, being musically inclined, learned to play it immediately, and whenever I close my eyes, I can see her in my mind's eye playing.

That ability showed me I'd be able to see her playing from the battlefield."

The commander nodded his head up and down, signaling he not only understood but also approved.

"When our young soldiers get homesick," Nghia said, "I hope hearing the memories of an older soldier will help them realize they are fighting for a good cause…the unification of their country. When this terrible war is over, and the two heartbeats of this great separated country beat as one, then I and my wife will also be reunited as one."

"Ah-ha, so after all, you do believe you will make it home," the commander blurted.

After a moment of humble silence, Nghia chuckled and went back to the part about his wife telling him what she believed.

"It's her belief, sir, but since we've been married for as long as we have, I have accepted what she says and don't argue with her."

Nghia understood that the war might be over soon and, then again, it could take longer. But whatever the time it took to run the Americans out, he'd stay on duty, willing to be away from his wife for the war's duration.

Those were the rules a northern soldier must agree to in order to fight the Americans in the south. A PAVN soldier could not expect to go home until the war was over unless the soldier was dead or had become totally useless. His wife also understood the rules and agreed that she'd wait for him as long as it took. She did not expect him to die, but she was prepared for that, should it occur, or at least she was prepared for a long separation.

Lieutenant Nghia was the party officer of his unit, but many times his role was more along the lines of an uncle figure, someone the younger troops looked up to and admired.

In this way, even though he still had to fight as the others, he could relate to the men because he'd been where they were, but at thirty-nine, he was older than most in the unit. He planned to share the poems he'd written on the Truong Son mountain range with the younger soldiers.

Late one night, a young soldier came to him with a request. "The commander told me you were a kind, understanding man, that you understood loneliness better than anyone in the unit." The young soldier wanted to know how that was possible, how the officer coped with the stress of war.

Nghia replied, "It's all in my memories. You have to think back. Of your family. Of your homeland and of how much you love it and what you are willing to do for them back home. In my case," Nghia held up his little book, saying, "My wife gave me this small book."

As the young soldier nodded that he understood, the officer began sharing the meaning of the little book. Besides being the most important possession he'd ever had in his whole life, he said this little book was actually his wife, and wherever he traveled, she would be there with him. Nghia said, "I've filled its pages with poetry, love poetry about her. She said if I'd do that, then each time I read the poems, she will be right here with me by my side... I need to ask something of you and the other soldiers."

"Yes, sir?"

"We are in a disastrous situation here. I cannot see myself getting out of this alive, but you are strong and young. You have the most chance. Therefore, I'm going to make a pact with you right here and now and with every soldier here. When I'm dead," Nghia continued, "you or one of the others who survives this war is to make sure this book gets back to my wife in Tai Giang village. You are to spread the word. Do you understand? Do you agree?"

"Yes, sir," said the young soldier.

"Good. Then we have a pact. When you honor it, you honor me, my wife, but most of all—our country. You also must know in return, as a memory of me, I gave my wife a flute," Nghia continued, holding his index fingers about eighteen inches apart, "that I fashioned from a piece of bamboo. She fascinated me each night playing the little instrument, caressing my heart through my ears. Amazing woman, my wife."

"But how does that help you right here, right now?" the young soldier asked.

"It's like this," Nghia said, "each night like tonight when everything is still and quiet, I imagine hearing my wife playing her flute. I can see her in my mind's eye, sitting on our patio playing my favorite tune. When she does, I am there with her by her side. That's what keeps me strong. That's what keeps us going. My memory of her playing while thinking of me is indestructible. No one, in the whole wide world—not the commander, not the Americans, not Uncle Ho himself—can ever take that away from me. I've written a poem about my wife…"

"I'd like hearing it very much, Uncle," he said, using that salutation rather than "lieutenant."

The soldier waited patiently as Nghia thumbed through the book's pages, searching for the poem.

"Here it is," he said once he'd found it. "I call it 'A Lullaby.'"

A Lullaby

Days, then months pass;
A year is twelve months, each with thirty
days.
You sit, numbering the days.
Fully six years have passed since I left.
That day your rosy cheeks were flush with
youth.
Their brightness still warms me.
The good old days lapsed into
Ongoing struggle.
At home, you still try to stay busy.
Autumn leaves have fallen six times since
I left.
You lean against the door, facing the river,
hoping.
You lift your gaze to the rosy clouds overhead.
You look around the yard, hoping
But still, see nothing.
The day I left, I promised
That I would return.
I will keep my promise.
You've lost yourself in tending the rice fields
Since the day I left 'til now.
At home, you are still daily hoping;
Your love is like pink silk.
How can I write all that I think of you?
You are a bird, feathered in lotus petals.
What could be brighter than the glow of us
together?
The greatest love is yours.

*As I lean against this light pole during
midwatch,
I gaze at your picture and return your smile;
So sweet is your expression.
Our love is like the sunrise
Shedding light through rosy clouds.
Missing me, you think up some verse;
With this pen, I will jot it down.
I am awkward; I don't know what to say.
How will I finish this letter,
My heart is bursting.
Though far apart,
The distance does not separate us.
We remain joined
In the spring of our lives.*

"Oh, wait a minute, did you hear that?" asked Nghia.

"Hear what?" the young soldier replied.

After a moment or two of silence, Nghia said, "I can hear her playing her flute right this moment. She's playing my favorite tune. It is music to my ears. It's beautiful."

After the faraway look on Nghia's face morphed into a smile, the young soldier heard him say, "Her music is what keeps me alive. Now go and think of your own memories and jot them down before it's too late."

As the young soldier rose to leave, he was reminded of their pact. The officer was dead serious: not "if" but "when" the war took his life, the little book was to make its way back to his wife in the north.

Although some of its contents were intensely personal, most were intended to be heard by Nghia's fellow soldiers, used to boost their morale. The younger guys would come to Nghia with problems, and, at other times, he would encourage them. He found that reading inspiring poetry aloud around a small fire at night was something the young men appreciated. So he recorded not only some of his own poetry but also some poems of others he found uplifting. The poetry in his book had been very special to the men of his unit. It expressed what was in all their hearts, and each time Nghia read the work to the others, often in the darkest moments between battles, his friends were deeply moved. They felt that nothing else so perfectly reflected their own feelings of why they were spending what might be the rest of their lives in the central highlands and jungles of the South. They felt Lieutenant Nghia's "diary" might be the only way the sacrifice of the average soldier could be understood by the people at home who never had been to war. They each took a vow that if Nghia was killed, one of them would carry the diary until the war ended, or it could otherwise be returned to the North. If that man were killed, another man would take possession of the cherished book. Then, ultimately, whoever was left alive would return the poetry to Thai Binh. They wanted the writing to be available within the village to serve as a memorial of the sacrifices so many of them had made.

A voice over the radio said helicopters were last seen flying north, carrying many troops. It was believed the unit could be the American First Cavalry Division, but they weren't sure.

The voice continued, "We know in the positive, the unit was observed walking into the Special Forces camp at Polei Klang. Sources predict the unit will be heading north, through the valley toward you, in helicopters. Troop numbers: more than a hundred. Advise your unit."

Nghia acknowledged the information and assured the voice on the other end they would be on the lookout.

Before nightfall, PAVN soldiers heard mortar rounds firing in the distance; they all agreed it could be the Americans.

THE BOX WAS IN OTHER HANDS

After several days of patrols in the bush near or around Polei Klang and having acclimated to oceans of green vegetation and rain, which no one ever liked, I was sent on a recon mission with a team of eight or nine others.

Not far from our company perimeter, no more than two hundred and fifty meters but of slow maneuvering due to dense, thick jungle and vegetation, we stumbled upon a secret enemy camp—often referred to by the enemy as a diversionary camp.

I stood near one of the entrances, scanning the land-scape—vertically, horizontally, left to right, up and down. In the middle, I noticed a mountain stream flowing with water from one end of the camp to the other.

When I bent over to soak my drive-on-rag (towel used around the neck) in the stream, my eyes followed the crooked stream to a pile of rucksacks.

The team leader, who noticed the neatly stacked back-packs about the same time, grabbed the radio handset from the radio telephone operator, "Alpha six, alpha six, this is Lima Six, come in Alpha Six."

"You got him," Davis replied. "Gimme a sitrep?"

"We've located an isolated, well-hidden enemy base camp only a couple of hundred, maybe two hundred and fifty meters from your location. We've got backpacks, beau-coup backpacks."

"Backpacks," Davis shot back, "you got backpacks. How many?"

"Roger that, six. Looks like about fifty-two, fifty-two as in foxtrot tango."

"All right, listen up," Davis said. "Leave everything in sight, except get the packs, get em' all, and get out of there now."

Back at their perimeter, the backpacks were all dropped in a not-so-neat pile. My platoon sergeant said they all had to be searched. After looking them over a few minutes, I became intrigued at finding out what things enemies carried, so I grabbed one and set it on the ground. With it wedged tightly between my knees, ready to have a look inside, I noticed both Capt. Davis and Lt. Doane headed directly for me. They were set on observing the backpacks' contents, like me, and, as I began untying its top flap, I got the idea everything inside belonged to me, but I soon learned differently.

*PAVN Rucksacks discovered on recon mission Captain Davis
conducted during the Battle of Hill 1064. Scott Murray (front)
and Specialist 4 Chapman search contents for information.
I (not in photo) garnered Lt. Nghia's diary from one of these
in the afternoon of March 17, 1968. Photo credit: Wendell
"Fritz" Schautz, Alpha Company 1/503d 173d Airborne.*

Right under the top flap sat two flags—flashes and
images of them hanging on my wall at home quickly dashed
through my mind, but Davis started screaming, "Gimme the
Viet Cong flag, Reed, gimme that VC flag!" while Doane,
managing to coerce me out of the other one, got busy with
a photo op.

One of two flags Lt. Nghia carried in his rucksack. Platoon leader Lt. John B. Doane displays the flag, Specialist 4 Chapman (far right) holding a photo of Ho Chi Minh. March 17, 1968. Photo credit: Wendell "Fritz" Schautz, Alpha Company 1/503d 173d Airborne.

I wasn't too concerned about them getting the flags because I knew I'd get more later, but suddenly the thought, *Something more valuable is inside,* came to me, and the flags were history.

As I reached into where the flags once lay, I found a plastic bag stuffed with several items. Through the almost transparent bag, I saw a few photos, military orders, an ID card, and, among other things, a small book covered in fake alligator leather appearing to be a diary. About the time I opened the plastic bag, a strong odor almost caused me to vomit. The plastic bag protected the contents from rot and mold caused by dampness and rain, but it also preserved sickening odors. I focused on the little book instead, and it helped avoid the odors.

Among things inside the bag, I saw what appeared to be a newspaper. Perhaps it was an enemy version of the

American *Stars and Stripes*, I thought. When I removed it from the bag, I couldn't read it, but I found a name I could, Ho Chi Minh.

Suddenly Chapman hollered, "Hey, look at what I got."

When I looked up, he was holding a large photo of Ho Chi Minh. I told him I wanted the photo. "No way," he answered, but at least my focus from strong, sickening odors coming from the bag had shifted back to what was inside the enemy backpack.

That's when the little book, with the alligator looking leather, came out of the plastic bag. Measuring about four inches high and three inches wide, the outside was covered with dried mud, but inside, its pages were clean and white as rice.

As I thumbed its handwritten pages, trying to make sense of what I held, I got the idea the little book could contain the life of an enemy soldier, from start to finish or at least present time.

That alone gave me the idea I was going to make it my own.

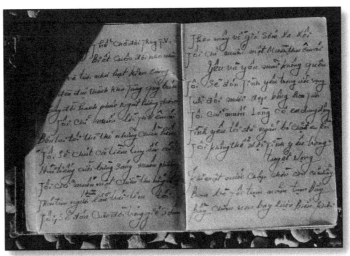

Inside of Nguyen Van Nghia's little diary.

I wasn't sure exactly what it was or what it would say if it could talk because it was in a language other than my own but holding the life of an enemy soldier was something that really pumped adrenalin. On this one thing, I was certain—enemy soldiers walked south on Ho Chi Minh trail five or six hundred miles to fight us. They had to be strong. Hardcore. Invincible. Capturing something like this was special, very special.

Also, in the plastic bag were papers appearing to be military orders. At the lower-left corner, a rubber stamp was printed in red ink. Twenty-fourth Battalion. 304th PAVN Regiment.

About halfway down the page, a name...

Nguyen Van Nghia.

"I hated him, that I know," I wrote in a letter to my parents. "I knew that much about him, and I hated all enemy like I hated him," I said. "He was just somebody I'd learned to hate and kill."

That night after guard duty, I made a small shipping box from an empty C-ration carton and placed everything inside. I scribbled my parents' name and address across the outside.

The next morning I made a full-throttle dash toward a supply chopper, but before I got there, the bird began lifting off. Then, the chopper lowered back down to a hover until the box came within inches of the door gunner and was snatched from my hands.

On the way back to my platoon, I considered different scenarios that might prevent the box from reaching my parents in the United States.

We were in Vietnam. In a war. In the middle of the jungle. Mail got lost. Boxes fell into rice paddies. Choppers got shot down, and door gunners didn't always come through.

However, I confided in at least one thing. The box was in other hands.

Ten days later, I received a letter from my mom: the box containing the small book had arrived.

CHERRY HILL

Early one morning, while most in his company ate rice, Lieutenant Nguyen Van Nghia sat atop one of the bunkers overlooking the valley to his front, guarding against enemy intrusion.

He had read about the Battle of Ia Drang and how the American First Cavalry Division used flying machines, but he'd never seen them before. Official army word for People's Army units like his was, "Do not be alarmed," as a victory against the American units using the flying machines was not only likely but probable.

Still, the sight of watching American troops disgorge from them as they sat down was not comforting.

Before hurrying off to report to his commander what he had just observed, he remembered reading what other PAVN units experienced while fighting the Americans with helicopters at Ia Drang. They said, "When you go south to fight the enemy, never forget you will be fighting invaders. They have enslaved your southern brothers and sisters and must be kicked out of the land. Take his food. Use his weapons. Remember, if you kill, he is dead, but if you wound, you will take two or three out of the fight. Stalk silently, attack from cover and in small groups. If you see you cannot win, leave quickly, do not fight, and do not be afraid of the flying machines. They only carry troops that can die from bullets."

"Come in, Lieutenant Nghia," the commander said from his underground office. The lieutenant climbed his way down, snapping a salute while saying, "Lieutenant Nguyen Van Nghia reporting as ordered, sir," holding his salute until it was returned.

"Ah, Lieutenant Nghia. I sent for you because I was looking over our bunker complex and noticed it needs better concealment, better camouflage. I want our position to be impossible for the Americans to find. As you know, we have established a diversionary position we can withdraw to in an emergency, should the enemy send artillery or try to overrun us. Still, I have a hunch the Americans will be arriving at this area soon, and I want our positions not to be easily found."

"They are already here, sir."

Locking eyes, the men paused silently.

The commander asked, "What unit do you believe the Americans have sent to meet their death?"

Nghia responded he thought they were the U.S. Army's First Cavalry Division.

"Why is that, Lieutenant Nghia?" the commander asked.

"Because the Americans used the flying machines in the battle of Ia Drang, and these have all come in helicopters, sir."

"Very well," the commander said, "we will give them the fight they are looking for, whatever unit they are."

"Send in Corporal Thi from the first platoon." *We will situate him as close to the Americans as possible without getting seen*, the commander thought to himself, *whatever direction they head.*

"Corporal Thi reporting as ordered, sir."

The commander returned his salute, "Corporal Thi, according to Lieutenant Nghia, the Americans have just arrived near our position. As soon as you see them setting up their nighttime perimeter, you are to notify us of that exact location, is that clear? Also, you are to take note of how many troops they have, how many radios, and how many are carrying CAR-15s."

"Yes, sir," Corporal Thi said as he saluted to leave.

Lieutenant Nghia was standing by when the commander asked him to retrieve their mortar crew sergeant.

"First platoon mortar corporal reporting as ordered, sir. The lieutenant has already briefed me. I understand I am to set up our mortar near the Americans on the southern trail closest to their position, is that correct, sir?"

"Yes, and when you get a call from Corporal Thi, you are to rain fire and death on the invaders. Remember, they are invaders occupying our land and must be kicked out, killed so they don't come back. Mortars spread a lot of shrapnel, do what bullets can't in a quicker time, you'll hit them hard and make them sorry they ever came to occupy our country, is that clear, sergeant?"

"Yes, yes, it is, commander."

The young mortar crew sergeant saluted and turned to leave but not before the commander spoke up. "Do you have a wife and family back in the north, sergeant?" the commander wanted to know.

"Yes, I do, sir."

"Then when you fight, remember you will be fighting for them and not only for our nation's reunification but also survival. The thinking in Hanoi is there are other countries that would like to take us over; to prevent that, we must fight and reunify, or we can be taken over by a different country. After reunification, we will be much stronger."

The lieutenant and commander watched him leave.

"How long have you been fighting for your country, lieutenant?" the commander asked.

"It's been three years now, but before I fought the French with the Viet Minh coalition for about eight years. Seems like all my life," Nghia said, thinking of his little wife.

Without further conversation, the commander told the lieutenant that time had come to send out a patrol in the direction of the Americans. The purpose of this patrol would be to draw them up the hill and lead them into an ambush.

"They will not all be killed but will call in their big guns and planes like so many times before. Now, this is very important, lieutenant," said the commander, "once they have burned the jungle with their firebombs and sprayed it with bullets from their aircraft, they will send in many men."

He continued, "You and half of your men will set up sniper teams on the hillside, wounding as many as possible, while the mortar platoon sends them welcoming packages with their names through the air."

Nghia saluted his commander and left.

He assembled his sniper team as he was told to do while keeping an eye toward the valley. In the distance, he heard bombs exploding. American B-52s were dropping bombs on the trail he and his unit traveled not long ago. In a flashback, he saw his PAVN brothers and sisters disappearing or being vaporized by B-52s. He had to shake off the images.

He thought to himself. *Go home, Yankees, to your families, so I can go home to mine. I never wanted to fight you in the first place. I'm tired of fighting in a war that we will never let you win anyway.* His thoughts were targeted to the Americans not only in the planes above but also to the ground soldiers coming his way. If they didn't go home and leave Vietnam, they would all be killed.

Later the snipers returned. "Report your successes to the commander," Lieutenant Nghia told them after he'd learned they had some kills.

"Corporal Quynh, regimental sniper reporting, as ordered, sir. We killed two Americans today."

The commander replied that he'd heard a lot of firing from M-16s. He inquired if their bodies were drug away.

As they spoke, the commander sought information on where exactly they were seen. "How far from our position did you locate the Americans?" he asked.

"We first noticed their point element and one other following him at about 500 to 650 meters to our west. Behind those, stretching all the way down the valley, appeared at least a hundred more. The two we killed were within 350 meters from our main bunker complex here. Others from behind moved forward and tried dragging away the bodies, but our continuous firing kept them pinned down, and by nightfall, they left. We got these things from their pockets," they said as they handed them over to their commander.

"This stuff is in English. I can't read it." Ah-ha! Now he understood Hanoi's wisdom in sending translators with the units.

"Go get Corporal Hung. This stuff is all in English."

"Yes, sir."

As Hung climbed down into the commander's office, he said he was reporting as ordered.

"Where did you learn to speak English, Corporal?"

"In Washington, D.C. at the University of America," he said, taking the items the commander handed him.

Corporal Hung looked them over. "An unsent letter and two military ID cards," he said.

"Very interesting," the commander noted. "Please tell me what names are on the ID cards."

"Yes, sir," said Corporal Hung. He studied a moment pronouncing their names as best he could. "Tremblay, Patrick J, and Blackshear, James G."

"What about the letter, Hung?"

"Letter addressed to America, sir. It has return address name and unit... Blackshear, James G, Alpha Company First Battalion 503rd Infantry 173rd Airborne Brigade, APO, SF 96250...whatever that means, sir."

"The 173rd Airborne, huh? Isn't that the same unit we humiliated not far from here at Dak To a few months ago?" the commander asked, not really sure he was correct.

He stared at the two ID cards and the return address on the unsent letter, trying to put two and two together when it hit him.

"That's it, that's it," he said out loud. "The helicopters Lieutenant Nghia reported seeing were not from the First Cavalry Division as our intel thought, they are the 173rd Airborne."

"They never learn," said the commander, "the more they send here, the more we kill."

Night fell.

About midnight, the commander was above ground checking on the men when he heard mortars exploding toward the tri-border area.

He had no way of knowing if the Americans were firing at a target or, he thought to himself, they could be letting everyone in the valley know they were awake.

Seconds before saying "Yes, sir," and turning to leave, the PAVN commander said to a sergeant on one of their bunkers, "we must kill as many as we can. We will be men and ammunition ahead and, hopefully, stop them assaulting our main position here.

"Remember, we must keep this path open to all our troops. We will cut a swath across South Vietnam from," shifting his eyes toward Laos, "Laos all the way to the South China Sea and take over the South. Also, you must not forget our actions here will ultimately divide the south, and the war will be won."

He continued with a word of encouragement, "We are winning this war. The Americans are weak, and after we kill all those who come near, the ones left alive will run like scared chickens."

The PAVN commander was about to go back underground when he said to the men on another bunker, "Anytime we can kill Yankee Americans, we get one step closer to reunification, and that's a good thing."

As the day made its way toward evening, Lieutenant Nghia scanned the valley to his west. He saw no movement, but there was a breeze. It was not much, but it reminded him of home, of his family, and his beautiful young wife, Vu. He removed the mud-caked little book from his shirt pocket, opening it while his thoughts remained fertile. On this day, he told himself, he'd pen something. It would be his remembrances of home. It went like this:

Returning North to Visit Home

The dirt road leading home is vermilion red, ablaze like my soul.

The echo of peoples' voices resounds from the empty ferryboat as the pigeons' coo lengthens. But the charm of the moment is lost in a homeland that stays divided in the heart of a separated lover who grieves for his broken country. One day of love spared

*for the motherland is worth a hundred years
remembering the roof on one's home.*
*Wind teases the green rice seedlings.
Corn on the hillside sways gently in the
breeze. The banyan tree in the front of
the coffee shop recalls the days when I was
young. The mossy lake with the long bridge
recalls the evenings spent fishing. Thatched
cottages, bordered by areca and bamboo
line the banks. Along with jackfruit and
banana trees.*

Lieutenant Nghia, thinking about what he had written, jumped to his feet when the commander came back above ground.

"With the Americans this close," he said to Nghia, who was standing near their ammo storage area, "put the troops on full alert."

Seconds later, a mortar slammed into the hill only about twenty-five meters to their front.

"It came from over there," one of the line soldiers said, pointing southwestward.

"Our mortar crew," the commander said, "get me our mortar crew immediately."

"Sergeant Cho reporting, sir."

"Sergeant Cho, you are to make sure your gun is zeroed here," the commander said, showing him the spot on a map.

"Lieutenant Nghia," he said seconds before returning to his office underground, "make sure men are okay in their bunkers."

Before Nghia could take three steps, complying with the commander's orders, another mortar round exploded, illuminating the entire hill.

Both surprised and shocked by the concussion from the exploding mortar round, he moved toward the closest tunnel, but as he was about to enter, another round hit and caused their ammo storage to blow with such force that it swept him from his feet and left him almost cut in two, helpless.

Reeling from pain, he reached for his stomach. The explosion ripped him wide open, exposing his intestines to rotten jungle stench and dingy bacteria. As he moved his hand down his leg, he felt a huge chunk of metal embedded in his upper leg, his leg dangling by a few pieces of flesh.

Now on the jungle floor and not being able to move, he heard more incoming. He tried crying out, but it seemed no one heard him above the explosions.

He tried stopping the blood by squeezing his flesh, but the pain was too much. He blacked out.

The Americans did not stop, they pounded his position relentlessly. Finally, flashes from the rounds enabled his fellow soldiers to catch a glimpse of his predicament: he was losing blood at an alarming rate and going to die if he didn't get medical care.

Between the incoming explosions, two soldiers carried the unconscious lieutenant down a winding trail to their underground hospital.

They left him and returned to their positions.

When Nghia woke, doctors had sutured his stomach, but they were about to amputate his right leg. He screamed, "No, don't do that! I need my leg! I need my leg!"

They argued with him that they had to amputate it, and he would lose it anyway. But Nghia wouldn't give in. He insisted they left his leg and, after a heated argument, they decided to do just that. "A leg without blood flow will not last long," they told him.

They screamed to the orderly, "Bring us a sizzling red hot metal rod quickly, quickly! Cauterizing the wound will only stop the bleeding," they said while motioning for the orderlies to hold him down.

As the doctor pressed the blazing metal through open flesh to reach the oozing artery, Nghia passed out from pain, but it was not before he let out a horrible, daunting scream. Once the bleeding stopped, the doctors were confident they'd at least saved his life, if only temporarily.

Moments later, Nghia regained consciousness again. This time he shouted to the orderly, "My pack! Where's my backpack?"

They were forced to tell him the Americans had been seen entering their diversionary base camp, backpacks were all confiscated.

For Nghia, already in the throes of death, getting the news his backpack was gone forever left him with no reason to live, but his memories of his wife were too concrete and undeniable to allow that to happen.

Yet, his emotions burned his insides, the pain of no longer having his little book, his wife by his side was no longer external but close to the center of his being, his heart.

Nghia screamed back at the doctors and orderlies, "The little book…it's all I had in the world. She meant everything to me."

They didn't understand. And he was too weak to tell them of her promise that she'd be by his side whenever he read poems about her. They feared the worst for him, not only that his little book was lost, but also his life.

Then suddenly, he calmed. It was as if she had never left his side as soon as he recalled a poem he'd written about her. He recited it to himself.

Remember the date we said good-bye, I saw tears in your eyes, and I can't say one word, even one word of love for you. You told me to remember to come home to see you. Six years pass along: no chance to come home. No chance to see you. The enemy still there with tanks, with jets, with warships. I must fight. If I lose, we will see each other next life, my darling.

SERVED BY DEPUTIES

I pulled my truck up to the trucking yard fuel pumps, and before setting the brakes, my boss showed up. He'd heard of the incident on the highway in Wyoming.

"Next time," he screamed, "next time something like this happens, you'll be fired," before storming off.

At home, my wife sent me an angry look as I stepped inside our house. She immediately hit me with the bills we had to pay but said we had no money.

For the past week, I had been strung out on sleeplessness. I was in no mood to argue over money, but the argument started while our young son was listening.

Silas rolled over and looked at me. The sad expression on his face needed no words. I kissed him goodnight and suppressed an angry flashback by staring out an open window and remembering one of my favorite country songs.

When I returned to the living room, Linda set her beer down, and the familiar argument resumed.

I looked over and said, "Look, I'm out on the road twenty-five days a month killin' myself trying to make a living, and all you can say is we don't have enough money."

"Oh, it's more than that," she said. "You need the road more than you need your family. Your son's growing up without a father. I'm living without a husband. Besides," she said, after taking a swig of beer, "there's something wrong with you. You're messed up in the head. I can't deal with it anymore."

"Oh yeah," I said. "Well, it's not me that's all messed up. It's you. You're the one that's taking pills and drinking like crazy."

At the beginning of our argument, like so many others in the past, there were just words, but this one turned violent when she slapped me. Refraining from returning the slap, I warned her not to do that again.

Then she came out with it. She wanted a divorce.

Young Silas watched his dad dive into his pickup truck and peel out.

As I was driving around, going nowhere, lights from oncoming cars threw me into a Vietnam War flashback.

Tracer bullets inches from my head streaked past, causing me to nearly lose control and head for the ditch. I heard the enemy mortars firing atop Hill 1064. I saw other Alpha Company men trembling as napalm tanks burst in flames at treetop level and remembered our trek upward in a torched and burned out jungle only to find dead enemy lying everywhere, even shallow graves where some had been buried.

Somehow I managed to park my pickup at the side of a nearby highway as the horrible noise and battle scenes faded.

I slept in my pickup until the sun woke me the next morning. I headed over to the trucking yard to check on another run to Canada. I was in luck.

My boss threw out a trip to Edmonton and said he had a load of Washington apples to be delivered to Texas from there. But first, my boss said, I had to load bananas at the dock in Galveston then take them to Canada.

"No problem," I said. "The truck will be backed up and ready to load early in the morning."

Trips like that usually took eight to nine days depending on the weather, but the extra time alone would let Linda cool down.

That night at the docks, another company driver named Nick Scoville got a huge, middle-aged lady of the night to beat on my door and wake me up as a joke.

I set straight up in the sleeper. Her beating on the door made me think I'd heard the thud of a mortar that failed to explode, a dud. When I looked out the window, I saw the overweight lady hanging on my door by her long, painted fingernails asking Nick, "You want me to climb through that little tiny hole?" referring to the hole in the back of the cab leading to the sleeper where I slept fitfully before all the ruckus.

I failed to see the humor and, almost always when awoken suddenly like this, came unglued, ready to fight like I was awoken so many times in combat.

Sitting in the truck next to mine at 4 a.m., Nick Scoville was laughing his head off. It wasn't funny to me, and I told him later over coffee I'd beat his brains out if it happened again.

I stood by the payphone in the warehouse, unloading the bananas in Edmonton, contemplating dialing home. I wanted to tell my son I missed him, and that I had to run over to Washington for apples, and that I'd be home in a few days, but the number was busy.

A week later, I pulled up to the fuel pumps of the trucking yard like I'd done so many times and set the brakes. I headed for the office, but a deputy sheriff intercepted me in the parking lot and served me with a restraining order saying I could not go near my house nor see my son.

The front door to my house was locked. The back door was locked too. But I could see Linda through the window. I beat on the window, demanding she let me see Silas, but she answered she was going to call the sheriff if I didn't back off.

I was on another run to Canada, but this time my truck had to get a load of citrus out of the Rio Grande Valley before heading north.

Sipping on a beer and playing darts, I was at a local Veterans of Foreign Wars meeting hall in the town where I was to load the next morning.

I complained to the other veterans about my wife and told them of my situation in general. The veterans talked about their outbreaks of anger, their inability to relate to others, and their difficulty keeping jobs or staying married. A few of them were Vietnam veterans.

If misery loves company, I had found mine.

One offered to help me find a place. Another gave me an attorney's number, and another wanted to know why I was so upset. He said he'd been begging his wife to leave for over twenty years, and she wouldn't leave. "You shouldn't be so disturbed," he said, "be thankful yours is leaving." Everyone cracked up except me.

Back in the truck yard, I was paging through the phone book and found a local attorney to discuss the divorce and the restraining order. I told the attorney I needed to see my son and was concerned with the amount of drinking my wife did.

The attorney assured me he would do everything he could to allow me to see my son, but once he learned how much I was on the road, he wondered how he could make a clear case for custody.

Several months passed, and I learned that my house was up for repossession. I went to see my son, and, oddly, Linda let me in. Not much time had passed when a new argument erupted.

"How come every time I call, the phone is busy?" I wanted to know, only to get back, "It's none of your business who I talk to."

"I've heard talk out on the road that you're dating someone. You're married," I told her.

"Not for long," she snapped back.

"Oh yeah, what's his name?" I wanted to know. "I heard it's one of the guys from the truck stop, a driver."

"Whatever," she snapped angrily and came at me, swinging. This time I hit her back, and it caused her to dial the sheriff.

Two deputies arrived and knocked at the door; they were invited in and immediately asked what the problem was.

Linda said, "It's him."

I said, "It's her. She's got a boyfriend while married to me."

She told the deputies I was a Vietnam War veteran, "He's crazy. There's something wrong with him."

"It's true," I told the deputies, "I am a veteran, and I endured some of the toughest, hardest, and cruelest fighting, but she thinks she's perfect. She's got worse problems, a log in her own eye the size of the moon."

Linda became heated and popped off in front of the deputies that she was going to kill me.

"That's not a good thing to say to a man in front of us," they warned her as they turned to me and began coaxing me to leave.

"Look," they said, "the best thing for you to do is leave right now…at least until this blows over."

I remained mute.

I'd had no divorce counseling, no preparation, no clear plan of action. My whole world seemed upside down. I didn't know what to do.

If I left, I'd have no place to call my own and might lose my son. If I stayed, I'd have to endure an unfaithful wife, which I could not accept.

I went after my shaving kit. When I returned, Linda observed, "Look at him. He's leaving," almost in a state of non-belief.

Both deputies studied me carefully and watched me open the door to my pickup and get in, leaving only after they saw me pull out on the highway.

But I found a spot to pull off the highway not far away and parked. The pain I felt was almost insurmountable, tears started to run down my cheeks. Inside, I ached, agonized, and felt a failure to my son.

This day was my tenth wedding anniversary. *Some anniversary* I thought, the wife threatening to kill me—and worse, the deputy sheriff's telling me I had to leave the house that my father and I spent countless hours building.

After a few moments to compose myself, I was back on the highway to a buddy's house, the buddy agreeing I could stay the night.

On the way there, I had a bad sign. I'd run a red light, only realizing what I'd done after seeing it through the rearview.

It was the same with my marriage: the fact it was over hit me once I was out the door, my house disappearing in the rearview.

I tried shaking it off by thinking about what the preacher said the last time I attended church, that the Lord won't put more on us than what we can handle, but it only helped for a minute or two.

TRAIL OF TEARS

At a field hospital not far from Cherry Hill, Nghia still suffered from his wounds when doctors said that they had done for him all they could. They prepared him to leave.

In essence, while he had a heartbeat and yet lived, his wounds were worse than those of the ones who had died, and due to malaria and other bacteria, he could not heal properly. His wounds might still be raw, they said, but he had to go.

As such, they helped him climb from the crude underground hospital to above ground where there was no security, only the jungle. The battle still raged the night they dragged him here, and doctors did not expect him to live. He remembered and didn't want to go there again.

Still, he had to leave even though doctors were fully aware he might collapse and die soon, but there was nothing more they could do for him.

There were no signs pointing "This way home" or maps, compasses, or directions. He'd been allowed to go because he had reached the third status of a PAVN soldier at war. He knew and understood the rules that no soldier would be allowed to go home except for one of three reasons:

No. 1: the war was over;
No. 2: the soldier was dead; and,
No. 3: the soldier had gotten wounded so badly they had become totally useless.

Nguyen Van Nghia had become totally useless to the war effort.

It meant, though he still might be able to walk, he was considered as good as dead, and while he never thought about dying in the hospital, he never really knew what kept him alive and for what future reasons.

Be that as it was, he was in the middle of a bloody war, and war was what he believed he'd return to should he ever recover.

The Americans would be seen in every direction, he told himself. He must be mindful not only of enemy ground forces but also of helicopters and jets with rockets and bombs. Yet, after a brief scan of the area with his one good eye and two good ears, he saw and heard nothing but familiar sounds of the jungle nearby.

Though he could stand on two legs, he hobbled as he lumbered along, favoring the leg he almost lost, to a position where he believed was the bunker complex his unit once occupied atop Cherry Hill, or Hill 1064 as it was known to the Americans.

It had been turned to dust by American bombs, artillery, and mortars. Foxholes and bunkers he helped his men construct were gone. Trees high above the tunnels they'd dug circling their defensible position had been blown away by artillery and bombs and reached toward the sky as giant toothpicks, still smoldering like the extinguished end of a cigarette.

The foremost thought at that moment, other than the eerie silence surrounding him, was that no one was there to greet him. He found no sentry, no defender, and no fellow countrymen as before.

They were all gone, and that was contrary to his remembrance the night he nearly got slashed in half by an American mortar round.

On this day, however, not only did he realize he was physically incapable, but he also discovered his unit had been decimated, doing nothing positive for its morale.

He was totally alone.

Before   the Americans attacked, he remembered peering through thick green vegetation. This time there was nothing like he remembered. No trees. No thick green foliage. No camouflage. He knew he could be spotted easily now, should the enemy fly over, and, unlike before, something was worse.

All his buddies had died. A smell—it was the stench of death.

He staggered as best he could to the shallow graves holding their dead who had been killed, rotting corpses of former soldiers he knew from the Truong Son trail. Jungle heat, maggots, insects, and dampness had begun absorbing them into the jungle floor, but their images were burned into his mind. While he stood saluting, he was uttering a solemn vow they'd never be forgotten.

Then his physical wounds became secondary, they were no longer his first concern. Moments earlier, while scanning for the enemy and trying to guess what direction he should take, he identified the area their diversionary camp had been.

What came to him then was a horrendous thought— the Americans had penetrated his camp, and his backpack was gone.

He remembered his wife's intentions, the reason the little book was given to him. She'd be right there by his side, she told him, whenever he read poems about her.

There was just one problem.

The little book was gone forever, taken by some American who was probably not capable of understanding its true value.

That thought caused him agonizing pain worse than from physical wounds, worse than getting cut to pieces during the American attack that ripped his belly open.

This time, the pain was not physical but emotional.

He realized when he lost his diary, he lost his wife and that she was no longer by his side, the same as if she had died. Now occupying the first place in his mind was not the agony of physical wounds, no. What hurt him was the emotional torment she was no longer by his side and the pact he'd made with a young soldier of getting his little book home to her was no longer possible. That alone caused him great anxiety.

But then, as he lingered in that depressing thought, he faintly heard her playing the flute he'd given her, and seconds later, a poem he wrote about her came to mind.

They were, after all, two people and only one heart, so he found out he could recite the poem the same as if he were reading. Immediately, he was calmed.

From then on, each time he found himself in those situations, he always turned to the poetry in his little book he had committed to memory, vowing that was how he'd keep his wife by his side.

Suddenly, he realized he'd have to wait for sundown to learn which direction he needed to go, so he rested.

Night by night, he stumbled along the jungle mountain trail toward the wife he loved, staying hidden during the day, knowing he could move faster and had less chance of getting seen at night.

He had nothing to eat, no fresh water, no medicine for his wounds, no change of uniform. He hobbled along, using a tree limb as a crutch, for days until he came to a village.

Unlike his abode in north Vietnam, the houses were on stilts. Off the ground, he suspected, because of monsoons.

A villager saw him hobbling along and offered help, but they couldn't understand one another. He drew a map of their two countries in the dirt, hoping the villager might understand what he wanted to know.

The villager pointed to an area of Laos, letting Nghia know he'd been going the wrong direction for nearly a month. But the villager, seeing Nghia was weak and wounded and in need of help, took him by the hand and led him to his thatched hut where he fed him and gave him a place to sleep for the night.

His goal was locating checkpoints in Laos. If he could get to one, to them, he'd find help and know he was going in the right direction.

At first light, Nghia had a fever. Relapse of malaria. The villager saw he was delirious, that he was in no condition to travel, so he did not let him go but nursed him back to health. When Nghia recovered his senses several weeks later, he was shocked to learn he'd been out for as long as he had.

After another two blistering weeks in the South Asian heat, he'd finally located one of his military's checkpoints. But everyone there had no time for him. Besides, the war still raged in the south, and all medical supplies were desperately needed there, leaving almost nothing for him.

Those traveling south were young and healthy as he was when he made the trek before, but he was forty years old now, weak and feeble from wounds, and had to use a crutch just to move. From his frail condition, those who bothered looking did not see how he could live another day, and worse yet, he was going where the trail got bombed every day.

He was nearly blind, delirious from malaria relapses, and he often lost his way. If it were not for villagers nursing him along, he'd have to give up, but he hopefully thought he'd get to the next village before another relapse.

Yes, he did remember everything good soldiers were supposed to remember during war, the part about never giving up, "We'll fight until the last bullet or last drop of blood, and we fight for unification and independence," but...occasionally, there were days he felt like giving up.

One day he came upon a dark, dark village. There were PAVN soldiers who lay dead. It was obvious there had been a battle, but with whom he didn't know. One had a pistol. He removed it from its holster and walked to an open pit, which he believed to be the burn pit of the village.

He put the gun to his head, thinking he'd just end all his misery and struggles, and pulled the trigger, but it didn't go off.

The gun was empty.

He went back for another bullet and went back to the pit. His finger tightened on the trigger. Then, seconds before pulling to put a round through his head, he heard something, causing his trigger finger to relax.

Tears came to his eyes when he realized it was his wife playing the beautiful flute melody he'd written a poem about in his little book.

The pistol now at his side, Nghia focused his attention not on giving up or dying but on Vu playing her flute and getting home to her as soon as possible.

Nghia spent many nights hobbling along many kilometers hiding, getting lost in the jungle, suffering from malnutrition, doing his best at listening for and avoiding tigers, blindness, lack of almost everything needed for survival. Still, there was nothing more important in the world to him than getting back to the woman he loved and having her by his side.

For months and months of hobbling from village to village and many malaria relapses, Nghia dreamed of getting a welcome at home if he could only get there. Then, finally, after two long years of hobbling along, he spotted his backyard patio in North Vietnam.

His wife, Vu, noticed him limping along and kept an eye on him as she believed he was not from their village. He was bent over and limped with a crutch, the one he made after doctors released him from the underground hospital. His form was similar to her deceased husband, and she tried picturing him as she remembered him years ago, but, *That is impossible*, she said to herself.

As she continued watching the man, she remembered her husband had been reported dead. *Never mind*, she still wished that were not so.

As the old man wobbled closer and closer to his patio, he recognized his wife immediately, and though she didn't appear to recognize him, she curiously kept watching him. *Doesn't she know who I am? Can't she tell I'm her husband?*

Nah, that can't be Nghia, Vu told herself. Years ago, when he left to fight, he stood upright, powerful, and was a strong man. A proud soldier in the People's Army of Vietnam. How could this weak, hobbling, and bent over old man be him?

But it was Nghia. As he neared their patio where she stood, she realized it was truly him. She'd been apprehensive and thought it was only his ghost, but as she touched him, she knew it was really him.

He was beyond exhaustion. His body reeled from old wounds, malaria, blindness, hunger, and malnutrition, but he still had enough energy to say, "Your flute. Your flute. I heard you playing."

"The army told me back in March 1968 that you had died fighting in Kontum," she said before they both dropped to their knees in an embrace seen only by newlyweds.

Her once strong and powerful man was now a far cry from what she knew him as before. In time, she learned the story of how his little book and papers were gone. They'd been taken by the Americans.

Now, her weak and hopeless man needed a lot of help. She got him to the doctor.

"He's got to prove his identity; he's got to have an ID before any treatment," the doctor hollered as he slammed the door in her face.

"That's impossible," she screamed through the door, "the Americans got his papers, and they are lost forever."

HOMELESS

I got a new driving job—hauling chickens for a wildcat truck operation between Miami and L.A. The truck had to avoid weigh stations, having no authority on highways in different states, I risked jail every time I evaded one.

One good thing about the job, though, it came with sleeping quarters—a bunkhouse. The small room, big enough for two twin beds and located halfway between Florida and California, became a place to lay my head between trips.

The place was a dirty, dusty old shanty that never got cleaned since it was built years ago. No plumbing, no running water, and no shower. My boss, Bill McAnally, looked me in the eye and said, "Real men do those things on the road."

Several months passed.

During one of my anger fits, I got mad at making Linda's car payments and decided to repossess it like the car lots.

It turned out to be another one of my bad decisions.

One trip later, Linda found the car parked outside the bunkhouse. She'd come to take it back while I was sleeping off a chicken haul.

She was almost gone and leaving when I woke in the middle of a bad dream. Still half asleep, seeing my car backing away made me think I was still in the bad dream.

When she saw me running toward her, she put the car in forward and mashed the gas, barely missing me, as I jumped under a tin shed.

I knew right then she had been serious like she said in front of the deputies, she'd kill me if she got the chance. *Gosh*, I thought, *And she says I have problems.*

McAnally got me a load of peanuts out of Gorman in west Texas for Miami. Once the load was delivered, I sat in a parking lot for a week, waiting on a load that never came, all alone and angry, with nothing but time on my hands. I got no pay for waiting, had no money for food, and was about as low as any trucker could get.

Miami was where I first tasted black beans. After a week of eating the beans and thinking about losing everything I'd worked so hard for and the thought of losing my son, I went into a depression and saw no way out. If there ever was a time to end it all, it was now, but after recalling someone once told me that it's a permanent solution to a temporary problem, and the fact it would hurt Silas beyond anyone's imagination, I let it go.

My whole life was about to boil over, I was in the process of losing my son, and I was stuck in some potholed and depressing parking lot where everything seemed hopeless.

Over the next few months, I ran back-to-back trips from L.A. to Miami. I got no rest or exercise and had no good food, slopping down garbage they sold as food out of old, outdated truck stops.

One thing I liked about driving trucks: there was no one looking over my shoulder telling me what to do. That one single thing, regardless of the dilapidated old diesel truck I drove, gave me an opportunity to find solace.

Time alone—for me at least—was best because around people, I found way too many opportunities to spring fights. One look at me the wrong way, I'd start swinging.

My father found me one afternoon in the bunkhouse in Texas.

"Your mother and I have thought it over," he said as he surveyed the small quarters where I laid my head in between trips. "We'd like to offer your old room to you until you can get back on your feet."

"Dad," I said to my father, "I'm a grown man. I can't move in with you and mom. I can't do that."

"You have no choice," my dad said.

"No choice, what do you mean by that?"

"You have a son. You must have a place where you can take care of your son."

I understood that I was in an uncomfortable fix. The house my dad and I had built was on the repossession list. The land it sat on was too. My job, in a sense, rather than making money, cost me. Then there were the nightmares.

As my dad was leaving, he said, "At least think it over and let me know."

Over several months, I realized I'd made a terrible mistake by leaving not only the house but also my son. With possession being nine-tenths of the law and Linda vowing never to give in, I feared she would use Silas as a weapon against me.

"No court in the land will give a child to a parent with no place to raise him," a driver at a truck stop told me.

I told myself that the man had a point, so I moved in with my parents.

Conversations at the dinner table were troubling. The grandparents got the notion their grandson was not in the best of care and that he could be in grave danger.

In motion after motion, I asked the court to give me custody of my son. "She's a bad person, your honor," I'd say, "my son is in danger with her."

But the judge refused.

He explained to my attorney that he'd personally interviewed Silas and found no evidence his mother was hurting him, so he wasn't going to move him.

That did not stop me. I vowed to continue fighting for my son like I had fought in the army, telling myself I would never, never, never give up!

Each of the three times I went to court, I reminded the judge about Linda's drinking, drug use, unstable condition, and emotional abuse of the boy.

The judge didn't see it my way.

In Texas, mothers usually got custody of the kids, and dads paid child support.

I kept kicking myself for walking out the way I did. Had I filed on her for abandonment when she left a while back, leaving the boy with me for over a month, the judge would see it quite differently, but he wouldn't budge now, so I had no other choice but to return to trucking.

Over the road, drivers had to call in each morning to let the dispatch know the load's expected time of arrival. During one of those calls one morning, I heard that I should expect to hear something of grave consequence.

After telling my boss when I expected to have the load delivered, he told me to call home right away: he'd gotten word something's happened.

"Linda's been involved in a serious accident," my mom said. "She's got head damage and is not expected to live. Can you get home right away for Silas?"

The highway patrolman who investigated the wreckage testified to the court. The boy's mother had been involved in a one-car wreck early in the morning. When they loaded her in the emergency vehicle, the patrolman told the judge alcohol was smelled on her breath. The man in the car with her at the time of the accident was arrested, taken to jail, and charged.

"After we smelled alcohol on her breath, we searched the car, her handbag, and the glove box. We found marijuana and two controlled substances in pill form along with a pistol with Reed's driver license number etched on the grip."

Seconds after the judge heard the officer's testimony, he hit the bench with his hand and said, "I'm reversing my decision. The boy goes with his father!"

Although I was pleasantly surprised to hear that, I knew that I hadn't won Silas, so much as Linda had lost him. I also believed that was not the last I'd hear from Linda.

Nonetheless, the grandparents were overjoyed. My son and I played catch in the front yard, a big change from what our relationship had been like in the early part of his life.

My prediction about Linda soon came true. My mother told me that she had called. When I returned her call, she said she wanted to pick her son up for a visit. I agreed, but only for a weekend.

She said she'd have him back on Sunday night.

Sunday night came, and he wasn't returned.

The following Sunday, no son returned.

Sunday week, still no son returned.

By then, my emotions were raw. I was taking a lot of heat from my parents. "Do something!" they said. "The boy may be in serious danger."

I tried to get some sleep but got none. Nightmares kept me awake, and I shook constantly at the thought of my only son getting harmed and possibly worse.

Every day, my anger toward her grew.

One day I got an idea. I'd call the only private investigator I knew: my first wife, who remained a friend.

She'd find him, she said, while asking pertinent questions. She inquired about his age, height, and weight and if I had his photos.

Several weeks later, she called.

My son had been seen in a grocery store not far from where he used to live. He'd also been enrolled in an elementary school; she had the bus number he rode home.

The next school day, I sat in the parking lot waiting beside the bus.

Suddenly, I saw Silas approaching, but I almost didn't recognize him. It had been several weeks since he'd had a haircut.

I barged onto the bus, expecting to be met by a vigilant driver, but there was none. The moment Silas saw me, fear twisted his face and made it almost unrecognizable, bringing memories of enemy soldiers captured during the war, believing they were going to die. He resisted me but only briefly.

In the car on the way to the grandparents' house, Silas asked what would happen to his mother.

I tried explaining, but he didn't understand.

I tucked my son in that night, saying everything would be alright and that I was glad to have him back again.

"You'll see," I said, "I'll make sure that things will be all right as soon as you settle in and get your routine."

Silas heard his dad with his ears, but his eyes told a different story. He didn't seem comforted.

A few weeks later, his mother came inside his school and searched from room to room for her son, and when she found his classroom, she entered it and attempted to remove him.

But she was stopped by the teacher and told to leave. She said she was not leaving without him.

The principal was called. Again, she was asked to leave but refused.

I got a call too and rushed to the school for an emergency.

Before I got there, security had been called. When Linda saw security after her, she sat down in the front of the classroom, terribly embarrassing the one she had come for.

When she wouldn't budge, the police were called. They removed her from the classroom by grabbing both arms and forcibly lifting while she remained seated with both arms and legs crossed.

Two police officers escorted her to their squad car and returned to the office for information. About the time they got to the office, she'd gotten herself out of their squad car and was on the loose in the school.

Officials from the school treated her interruption as a terrorist attack. While the police attempted cornering her, school officials ushered all the remaining kids out through emergency doors.

While she wrestled, kicking and screaming, I had a paranoid flash, thinking the worst. Nightmares suddenly became real and hit me in the face. I began shouting to the police that she had a gun. My voice echoed up and down the halls. Kids, parents, and faculty heard my screams and ran for cover.

Finally, the police slammed her to the floor and searched for weapons. They found none, but she was escorted again from the school but this time in handcuffs.

Silas stood alone in the hallway, watching everything unfold with tears streaming from his innocent, tender, little face.

At dinner, the boy couldn't eat. He sat across the table and just stared at me. I felt about as low as anyone could go when he broke his silence and asked when he'd see his mom again. Hearing that crushed me, but I knew he didn't realize he'd been rescued from a lot of hurt and pain.

As I tucked my son in that night, I told him, "Things will be all right; mommy means well, but she has some problems she needs to deal with before she can spend time with you."

Silas began to cry, saying he missed his mommy and that he'd rather be with her than me.

I exploded, taking all of my pent-up anger and aggression out on him.

I finally stopped, but it was too late: the damage had been done. Silas was already upset at having been taken from one place to another with no say, and my outburst only made it worse.

Later that night, I jumped in my pickup truck and headed to a local truck stop, seeking the comfort of familiarity.

Two truckers sat with their girlfriends a few booths away, making too much noise and having too much fun. A fight broke out.

Back home, I nursed two black eyes and wondered how to explain them to my son in the morning.

BACK IN THE NORTH

Vu Thi Gai was visibly upset. Her husband needed medical care, but doctors denied him. He was a career military man due a pension, but the government denied that as well. No one in the province could get those benefits without proper identification. His wife found out he would have to prove his family tree, place of birth, including the year, and also provide military records showing he'd been in the military before the government would treat him or provide any military pension. Yet he had nothing, no papers of any kind.

"Surely there is something you can do for him," Vu told the People's Committee chairman, "Can't you see he needs help? He is a weak and wounded man," raising his shirt and pointing to terrible scars across his stomach and leg.

"Yes, of course, I can see those," he replied while studying the disfiguring scars. "But my hands are tied. We've run into this situation before, and he'll have to prove who he is in court to get his proper identification; that's the rules. Once he's done that," the chairman told her, "he can get new identification papers and get on with his life. Until then, he'll have to get along as best as he can, the same as any other person in the province."

Back at home, Nghia felt frustrated by his wife's failed efforts to get him the care he needed and struggled with the idea of telling her of his war experiences, though he didn't really know how. But he hoped if he told her, she'd at least focus not so much on the doctors and committeemen who were rejecting his request for the things he'd earned but on the Americans and the war that caused him all this grief. Once she understood, it might calm her resentment toward their government workers, he reasoned.

He explained his struggles during the years he was away as best as he could, starting with his trip south on the Truong Son range where the little book she'd given him years ago first came into the picture. His story took her across streams and above tall mountains, forging deep rivers on a journey that always forced them to watch for the enemy's huge guns and huge bombs. There was never enough sleep, enough food, or enough medicine, never enough hours in the day to cover the kilometers their leaders demanded. They were exhausted all hours of the day and night.

At home, he wasn't upset with local doctors or the People's Committee for getting denied the services and things he'd earned, he'd gone years without those things in the south, yet the war raged on, medical supplies and money should not be spent on anyone not qualified.

He wanted his wife to understand how fortunate he was to be home, though weak and seriously wounded. When he tried so intently to tell her, the effort caused him to choke up. Head down, Nghia tried to hide the tears, but she pulled his chin up with her index finger and looked him in the eyes. She loved him very much, and she was happy he was home and back with the family, she told him. It was the warmth, soothing, and caressing he'd missed the last several years.

He was grateful she played the little flute he'd given her, he told her through streams of tears. "I heard you playing many times." When she perked up and asked, "Really?" he confided it was only his imagination, but in the end, it still got him home.

She knew his papers and the little book she'd given him went missing, but she said it was more important to have him home alive without those things rather than him being dead with them. That was her personality. She was the best companion he could ever hope for, and he reassured her while making her a cup of hot tea as they got ready to retire for the night.

The next morning after a restful sleep, they were off to see friends who also had soldiers in the war and wanted to hear a fresh report of how the war in the south was going. The son of their closest friend had joined the army and had gone south to fight, but they hadn't heard from him going on five years.

"My wife only heard from me once in five years," Nghia told them as signs of deep sorrow covered their faces regarding their son.

Vu Thi Gai told them about the little book. She told them of her husband's gift of writing poetry and about giving it to him before he left to fight. She believed both he and the little book would return to her one day, their friends learned.

Amazed that her husband returned as she had foretold, they were curious. "But what about the little book? Has it also returned as she stated?"

Nghia spoke up. "It was lost in the jungle," he said quickly while glancing toward the door. They sensed he didn't want to relive the little book's loss but said another time might be best. Something stopped him at the door and he came back, insisting he'd stay and tell them the details anyway.

They were anxious to hear because they had not traveled great distances as he had, and they mentioned they were happy he had stayed. After a while of talking, he came to his unit's diversionary camp, the place where they stored backpacks and ammo, used as a retreat to keep the Americans off-balance.

To help them understand the principle behind diversionary camps in battle, he explained cooking without smoke as an example because they all understood eating and cooking. In the jungle, that was very important because helicopters could see white smoke against a backdrop of green jungle easily and fire on them.

Because of the smoke, they cooked underground. They dug tunnels or long vents just under the crust of the earth's surface, leading away from where they actually cooked. The underground tunnels transferred the smoke to another area by as much as a hundred meters or more.

He didn't say that smoke didn't rise from the trees; it did. But the location the smoke rose was a long way away from where they cooked, helicopters firing at smoke over there would miss the camp, and soldiers could live yet another day.

But they didn't always have to worry about cooking rice and making smoke, he told them. With a somber expression on his face, he said sometimes there was nothing except tree roots to eat.

About that time, Vu cleared her throat and interrupted.

"When you left, dear husband, you were only missing one incisor tooth, but now you are missing the one on the other side."

Nghia had lost the first one on the left during the French war. She knew about that one. What she didn't know was how he lost the other one on the opposite side.

"Oh," he chuckled, "that one got whacked out under the same circumstances. A soldier backed into me on the Truong Son range trail," he told them. Now, he was missing two teeth. One lost during the French war, and the other the American.

After they chuckled a moment, he scratched his head, wondering if they understood the principle behind the cooking without the smoke story, that is, not just the reason, but how it saved lives.

Because in the story, he was about to let them in on, the principle was the same—they saved lives by keeping the Americans off-balance.

"We believed, because our diversionary camp was well concealed, the Americans could never in a million years locate the camp. That's why we stored our gear there."

"Ammo, hospital supplies, and, of course, our backpacks." He repeated, "The Americans were never supposed to find that camp."

"The diversionary or camouflaged camp, as our commander liked to call it, was between two mountains and extremely difficult to find, especially for those clawing their way through the jungle. It was naturally hidden and nearly impossible for helicopters to see because of tall, thickly bunched-together trees.

"Only two to three hundred meters from our main battle positions, the camouflaged camp was easy enough for everyone in the unit to locate. Sometimes there were emergency drills, practice runs between battle positions and the camp. They timed the fastest runners to learn how long evacuation might take if artillery comes," Nghia said.

"Inside, it had many comforts of home: a fresh water stream which meant water for drinking and uniform washing, shade from the sun's dreadful heat, plenty of trees for our hammocks, and stair steps leading up one side of the camp's mountainous slope."

One of the people broke in, assuming he'd add a little humor to lighten the story, "That sounds like an oasis of peace in the middle of a war zone," he said, but then realized it was not funny after they shared the look he got.

"During the battle for Cherry Hill that we occupied, somehow the Americans had gotten into our diversionary camp. Our camp was meant to keep the Americans off-balance. I only found out about the Americans getting into our secret camp while I was in the underground hospital," Nghia said before pausing.

Suddenly one of the neighbors wanted to know why they called the hill they were on Cherry Hill.

Nghia cleared his throat and said, "We occupied a hill that was part of a cluster of hills named that after an earlier battle. Both blood and cherries are red; the cluster was the location where the blood of thousands and thousands of PAVN soldiers got spilled."

After a moment of reflection, he got back to the part when doctors were about to amputate his leg, "Doctors told me then that our backpacks had all been taken."

But when he explained that everything he owned, everything he cared about, and everything worth fighting for was in his backpack, he broke out into tears, and they sensed he lost a part of his soul that day.

"The Americans were not supposed to find the camp," Nghia blurted emotionally, with a raised voice. "It wasn't just a dirty old, sweaty backpack containing flags, photos, identification papers, and news articles from Hanoi," he said while trying to disguise his true sorrow of losing the little book, but the tears falling from his cheeks told a different story.

"Something more painful than death," a tearful Nghia said, meaning, "When Vu is no longer by my side." A curious look came over them.

His backpack was gone forever, he said.

The part about his wife prophesying that both he and the little book would return to her could no longer be possible.

CHAT WITH GOD

McAnally called, saying he had a load of chickens for Albuquerque.

The good thing about the job with his trucking company, I was able to attend Wednesday night prayer service at my church fairly regularly, so I headed to the chicken farm to pick up the load.

As it was in the military, my personality didn't always blend with others. Such was the case of a man named Tony Bagwell.

Much of the time, he came off as abrasive, overpowering, and forceful in what he believed about God and how everyone should have his same beliefs.

What the heck, I thought. I was out of the military and wanted no part of being told how or what to believe.

Unfortunately, great friction and confrontation developed between Tony and me, and each of us showed discord and dislike, if not outright hatred for one another.

At first, we tried hiding our dislike and disrespect for one another, but eventually, others noticed it, as we would not so much as speak.

On Sundays, if one of us saw the other heading down one aisle, we would suddenly move toward the aisle on the opposite side—anything to avoid a face-to-face approach where we would be forced to speak.

When it seemed there would be no end to our petty behavior, I found a new church home, but after several months, I moved back.

Before long, our hatred for each other became common knowledge in the town where we both lived. As God-fearing men, we both knew that kind of behavior would not be accepted, but our pride kept us from any kind of reconciliation.

On the road to Albuquerque, about 1 a.m., my truck rolled along at better than a mile a minute when something unexpected happened. I had been thinking about getting the load off as quickly as possible and heading back home when suddenly I felt my heart beating faster than normal.

Then over the next few moments, the beating became stronger and stronger, until finally, I felt like my heart would explode.

It was true I had been on the road a lot lately and was tired, but there was no explanation for what I was experiencing as it had never happened before. I could not understand the sudden surge. Perhaps I was not supposed to—I didn't know, but I *did* know at that precise moment in time, my heart was racing like never before, and the feeling that came over me along with the surge was joyous, definitely something out of the ordinary for a tired trucker.

Suddenly like a volcano ready to blow, out of my mouth came words I never thought in a million years I'd be hearing myself say. I said, "I love Tony."

I would never say that, so it wasn't me. It had to be God making a statement that He loved Tony because I definitely would not say anything close to that. But then, out it came again. I repeated that statement two more times, and with each utterance, I became more and more amazed by what was happening. By the time the urge causing me to emit such a statement had ceased, the hate and bitterness I had for Tony had been replaced with love and warm thoughts of joy for him.

It happened so fast. *What was that?* I asked myself.

If I hadn't heard it with my own ears, I never would have believed it, but from my own mouth, those words came. Still, I had to ask, *What caused this?*

A friend once told me God spoke through many things, including birds and animals, but for some reason, I was reluctant to believe it had happened to me.

After thinking a few moments, however, I was convinced. It was the voice of God speaking through me. Indeed, God had spoken by using my own vocal cords when He said, "I love Tony."

That didn't come from *me*. I knew that, but I still heard my mouth saying it. My ears heard it. My heart felt it. In the time it took my truck to go five or six miles, I knew it was real and a far cry from where I was only moments before, but I was delighted: my heart was singing a new song toward Tony.

Keep the truck between the white lines, I told myself. The highway into Albuquerque was downhill now, and the city's lights could be seen when I became curious why I'd received a supernatural communication.

I'd read about imputations in the Bible. How someone's heart was opened up, and information poured in.

That was what came next. There was no audible voice this time, but the communication was more like receiving a radio signal internally. The signal came in loud and clear, informing me that Tony and I were great friends.

"Huh?"

Yes. Your relationship with Tony has been fixed.

I was stumped, dumbfounded, the better word. It was one thing to love the man, but to learn the slate of everything between us in the past had been wiped clean now was almost unbelievable, considering how long Tony and I had been prone to fighting.

In an effort to be sure what I heard was not fake or unreal, I spoke up audibly as if someone were with me in the truck, though a quick glance revealed no one. "What is this all about?"

The signal continued: *When you get home and go to his house, just walk in like you are family. You no longer have an enemy in Tony. Just walk into his house.*

I was both shocked and amazed but also skeptical because Tony was a large man. I'd do it anyway when I got home.

My mind spun as fast as the miles passed. Arguments between Tony and I came to mind. How could the two of us become friends? I understood there had to be a reason this was happening. There had to be.

Both hands on the wheel, grabbing gears, with white lines passing ever so fast, my ten hours of driving duty were almost up when I saw the sign. Albuquerque was only a few miles more.

I had heard from Heaven above, and God spoke through my own voice, letting me hear an audible and penetrating message. Indeed, my heart had changed. I'd moved from hate to love for a former enemy. A miracle. It had to be, but there was more. What was the purpose behind receiving this?

Why on this date, on this highway, at this time of night, was I imputed with love for my enemy-turned-friend?

After a short pause, the answer...

Tony will not be around much longer.

With the exception of wind, humming wheels, engine RPMs moving up and down, gears shifting...the cab of my truck went silent.

I received a signal like on the radio, and as instantaneously as it began, it stopped. This was serious. It wasn't just the message that Tony would be going out of town or moving to a new church, it carried a very deep, profound message…

Tony would not be alive much longer.

I backed into the dock where they received shipments of chickens and set the brakes. During a phone call two hours later, McAnally said he was not able to find a load, and I had to deadhead back.

While lunching at a local truck stop just outside town, I got the idea to put the truck in the wind; if I hurried, I could make it back in time for Wednesday night's prayer service.

Prayer service had already started; I'd almost gotten there in time, only about ten minutes late when I entered our church building and sat down. Pastor Terry had already opened the meeting with prayer and asked if anyone had a testimony or prayer report.

Apparently, Tony Bagwell had one; he was already at the podium. No one had a clue, but I was starting to perceive something unexpected, though my hope was that it was not what I had learned the night before. Tony spoke of family, the importance of families, and the meaning of life as he saw it, including other families and people outside everyone's families.

Then, he shifted to a new subject. He'd been to the doctor and had an announcement. At that point, a pin dropping to the floor could be heard.

Then *boom*! The announcement. He had cancer.

He wasn't seeking sympathy, tears, or even sorrow, he said, and before that hit anyone, he continued he only had six months to live, but he reassured everyone he was solidly in God's hands.

Shortly after leaving the podium, Tony wanted to be baptized. In the stillness of that moment, I said I did too. We were baptized together.

Still dripping wet in the little room behind the baptistery, we each confessed how badly we had treated one another and began laughing at how stupid our little charade was. Tony said he wanted forgiveness, and as the two of us forgave each other, we became friends—exactly as had been foretold.

While we both laughed at corny jokes about things or the stupid thoughts we had toward one another, Tony blurted out that he loved me.

It caught me off guard then slowly brought tears to my eyes. I was extremely thankful heaven made this all possible while letting Tony know that I loved him, too.

Not long afterward, Tony could no longer swing a hammer. He and his brother were carpenters, but the treatments made working impossible.

More than once over the next several months, I would leave the Sunday church service a little early on my way to the parking lot, where I'd place hundred dollar bills in Tony's car and wait inconspicuously in my car nearby.

Tony would spin around when he saw the money wedged in his steering wheel, trying to see or figure out who the gifter was, but he never caught on—that way God got the credit, but the real thrill for me was watching him in the rear-view during that sweet moment of joy as he bowed his head in thankfulness.

Six months later, almost to the day, Tony died.

I was thankful God didn't let the man die with the kind of hatred I once had in my heart for him. I just hadn't known the real Tony.

NGHIA'S WAR EXPERIENCE

After taking them through some of his most painful memories about Vu no longer by his side, Nghia changed the subject.

The most frightening part he recalled was not only American artillery but also the sight of his fellow PAVN soldiers clutching death on nearby Truong Son range.

"B-52s flying high overhead, no one heard them, suddenly soldiers vaporized before my eyes." The images, pictures of entire regiments disappearing into huge clouds of dust, wouldn't go away.

Vu watched his eyes, tears began forming, and before they dropped, she reached to wipe them from his face hoping to erase some of his memories, but she knew from her personal experience that might not be possible.

As much as Nghia may have wanted to forget, he brought home things that were even more painful. Nguyen Van Ba, his younger brother and a favorite among his siblings, died in the fighting at Kontum. As far as Nghia understood, his remains had never been recovered. Ba got no proper burial, no last ceremony, no recognition, and no posthumous medals of any sort. He was just dead, presumably melted into the jungle or turned to mist by huge bombs. Nghia, acting in the early family traditions set forth by his parents, lit several candles and, content to stare at them until the flames disappeared, told Vu he would not hold a grudge against those who took his brother's life.

Vu knew and understood the heartache flowing through her husband's being, as she had experienced her own tragedy. She was only two out of eleven brothers and sisters who survived starvation during the Japanese occupation of Vietnam during World War II, unfathomable even by Vietnamese standards, but years later still very vivid in her mind.

Once the candles gave in to the night, the two, after making sure their children were all safely in bed, settled in for the night, confident the sun would come out in the morning, bringing a new day for which to be thankful.

Early the next morning, as the sun first began showing itself, Nghia and Vu sat under their banana trees sipping tea when a man from their local People's Committee approached.

"Good morning, are you Nguyen Van Nghia?" the man asked.

When Nghia answered he was, the young man introduced himself. He was To Quang Hang of the Tien Hai People's Committee.

Nghia had a pending court date; the court was giving him an opportunity to get identity papers so he could start receiving medical care and his military pension, Mr. To said to Nghia.

Vu spoke up and said that was good.

"What kind of evidence does the court want to see?" Nghia asked.

"Your birth records, proof of your family, photos, anything that can document you are who you and your wife say you are," the runner answered.

"But how can that be possible?" Vu said, "The big typhoon a year ago flooded our house and destroyed everything we had like that."

Not knowing how to answer, the man named To remembered he was only the messenger and departed without answering.

Not long after her husband's homecoming, in the middle of darkness, Vu had woken him along with their children and forced them all to run after she heard the announcement that American bombs were coming.

In pitch darkness, they ran and stumbled as an American bomber screamed overhead. "Those barbarians," Nghia said to her. "We are only a small country. Why must they bully us this way?"

She didn't have the answer but said, "We must get to safety quickly before they kill us all."

When they reached bomb shelters built for inhabitants of their village at the beginning of the war, Vu bravely stood at the door, ushering them inside before entering herself.

This was not the first time Nghia had been in shelters that he and his fellow soldiers called bunkers back in Kontum, but it was his first experience being in one this close to his home, with his wife and children. He couldn't recall how his wife knew they had to get up and run in the middle of the night like that, as she claimed she'd done many times, so he asked her how she knew.

"The Russians," she said. "They have ships off the coast of Okinawa and Guam, and even spotters in Thailand that radio Hanoi whenever the American bombers take off. We know before the bombs start falling how much time we have to get to the shelters, the loudspeakers alert us." She said she and the children had run to this exact shelter on many occasions, as many as three times in one night.

Yet, this time in a shelter, her husband was not a healthy, strong man as before. This time, he was a weak and wounded man accompanied by his wife and children, who huddled around him, attempting to comfort him as memories of bunkers atop Cherry Hill flooded his mind.

Again, as he did on the battlefield in Kontum, he turned to poetry to give him, his wife, and their children some comfort as they heard exploding bombs rocking their small village and feared for their lives.

About that time, he spoke up. He told his wife of a poem he wrote about her flute, as dirt from the earthen walls fell on them, as huge bombs fractured the earth only a few meters from them, outside. "During one of my darkest times in the south fighting the Americans," he whispered, "this poem reminded me of you and gave me comfort. It's called 'The Flute.'"

He started reciting from memory, then paused, "I forgot to let you know, I wrote it as if it's a conversation between you and me and," and then continued, "It goes like this:

The Flute

'Last night beside the fire, I stayed up all night. I made this flute for you, my love. Until we meet again, may you see my face each time you play. Remember our promises to remain forever faithful. I can see you playing the flute constantly. Though far apart, you will always be waiting for me.'

'My love, you joined the army to serve your country. Troubled, I yet advised you to defend your native land. We embrace, oh my dear. Never embrace another. Please always remember the flute you gave me. Remember our promises to remain forever faithful. Though far apart, I will always

be waiting for you. I stand here in the rice fields at day's end; mist clouds the horizon.

'My little flute melody has been carried off by the wind. It is for the one I love miles and miles away. The rice shouts with glee in the fields. The blooming flowers renew my hope. I sew this shirt with my love to send to my faraway soldier. Though far apart, I will always be waiting for you. I am always with you.'"

"Oh, my dear, dear husband," Vu said, "here we are in this bomb shelter together with the children. We only know the bombs are falling, not if we live to love again, and as the bombs yet fall, shaking the earth around us, they have not shaken your memory of me."

An announcement came over the loudspeaker. The bombing planes had left. It was safe to return home.

Once the sun came up the next day, Nghia, Vu, and their children surveyed the area around their house for damage but found none.

That was not the case for a military installation several hundred meters from them. They saw huge bomb craters and collapsed buildings in every direction they looked, but fortunately, their local People's Committee building survived the bombing with little damage.

As the date Nghia had regarding his identification papers hearing at the People's Committee office that survived the latest bombing raid approached, he and his wife concentrated on what the man had earlier told them to bring.

Suddenly, Vu said he should visit his military unit. He replied the war was still going on and that they still fought the Americans in the south, so that was not a good idea.

The next morning, Nghia was helped by Vu into a wagon full of rice stalks going in the direction of his old unit.

It'd been years, but he recognized the building, remembered the surroundings where he had taken the training, but it appeared vacant. There certainly were no soldiers as before. There was, however, a man inside.

After knocking on the door and hearing, "Come in," Vu helped her husband hobble in and stand before the man.

"Good afternoon, I am acting regimental Colonel Han. How can I help you?"

Nghia, feeling awkward, didn't know how to begin, but Vu did. She told the officer, as best she could, their names and of her husband's loss of his identity papers while the colonel carefully eyed them both up and down.

"Oh, is that right?" the man said curiously after hearing her say Nghia had joined this unit going south on the Truong Son range to fight the Americans.

"Well, how can it be he is here alive, and the war yet rages? You know," the colonel screamed at the pair, "there are only three reasons a PAVN soldier gets out of fighting! But your husband is here, alive, claiming he fought the Americans where many of our countrymen became martyrs. How can that be?"

Vu, seeing that she might have made a bad suggestion that her husband come there, ripped his shirt open, exposing his horrible wounds.

As the colonel stared at Nghia's wounds that had not properly healed, she asked her husband to remove his pants, revealing a leg wound that was as good as an amputation.

"When he was wounded, he was taken to the underground hospital and, not expected to live, dismissed as totally useless to the war effort. These wounds are what my husband did for the war effort, Colonel Han. He cannot work, take care of our family, or do any of the things he did as a strong and capable man as before. Must we be punished more? Can't you see he needs help?

"Doctors believed he'd die on the Truong Son range. How he made it back to me, I have no sense of understanding, but he is here, and doctors will not treat him in our village unless he has proper identification papers that were lost in Kontum while fighting the Americans."

"I see," said the colonel. "In that circumstance, let me search the unit roster."

The colonel returned, he'd found her husband's name, but according to the records, Nguyen Van Nghia died in 1968 in Kontum.

She said, "Yes, that's right, the military men came to my work letting me know my husband had been killed while fighting the Americans, and I grieved and grieved. But two years after that, he showed up at our village."

"Very well," the colonel said, comparing the scar above Nghia's left eyebrow to the information in his records, "I'll furnish him with information suitable for the People's Committee court; he can get new official identity papers and medical treatment."

Nghia went to court and got his official identification papers restored. He began medical treatment for war wounds and started receiving a military pension. During a medical exam, a doctor found many health problems, including his vision impaired in one eye and not as good as a man his age should have had in the other. Unfortunately, the doctor informed both Nghia and his wife they had neither the experience nor the equipment to remedy his eyesight problems.

POLLY AND THE BOX

When the dust settled after getting my son, I found myself in a new place. Homeless and penniless. And since I was now a stay-at-home father, I had no hope of returning to driving any time soon.

This meant menial jobs for cash and barely enough for coffee. Yet I had faith things would improve, never knowing how or when.

Mostly, I would push the issue of homelessness from my mind: a practice called "stuffing it," learned in Vietnam. I did not realize I was suffering from PTSD (post-traumatic stress disorder), a symptomatic emotional condition. At first, the condition was labeled The Vietnam Syndrome, but Soldier's Heart, Shell Shock, and Battle Fatigue were the names for the condition during the Civil War, World War I, World War II, and Korean Wars. The condition became properly labeled as PTSD after the Vietnam War.

Whatever the label, its symptoms were disruptive. In mechanical drafting class in high school, I made straight As and even A+s. My instructor recommended a career as a graphics engineer or an architect. My drawing ability was that good.

That had been before PTSD, but this was now. Sitting still was the requirement for draftsmen, engineers, or architects, and going back to high school days to pick up where I left off was no longer possible.

It was Independence Day in 1989 when I took a friend to the Cotton Bowl to see the annual Fourth of July fireworks display. We arrived during the early evening hours and saw a large display near the front gates. It appeared to be a stack of red Texas granite blocks on a plywood platform, and as the two of us approached, I saw hundreds, perhaps thousands of names. The names were part of the Texas Vietnam Veterans Memorial. The new memorial was to be officially dedicated on November 11 of that year—Veterans Day.

I did not try to read the names or look for buddies who died, as it appeared other visitors were doing. Instead, I got hit with what felt like a brick to the head. Suddenly, I was swarmed by emotions I didn't know existed.

I felt my chest constrict like an elephant was sitting on me. I gasped for air as tears flowed uncontrollably down my face. I turned and ran, not knowing where I was going, nor what I was doing, nor why.

Vietnam came to the forefront of my mind standing at the wall. Seeing it for the first time shattered my already frail state of mind.

As my friend approached me, I was unable to express what was happening or even think logically. It was like experiencing the horrors of war all over again on a videotape revealing the deepest aspects of my being. Not just an audio/visual record of the past.

I saw nightly television news coverage of the early years of the war. People dying, though in a dispassionate way, much like watching a war movie on television.

I recalled to memory newspaper articles, remembered protesters saying that too many people were dying, and I remembered the politicians talking about the "domino effect."

After experiencing the war memorial, the only thing I could focus on was the war in Vietnam. Counselors at the veterans centers said the more I talked about it, the less an issue it would become and the less focus I would have on Vietnam. I got invited to speak at high schools seeking personal experiences of Vietnam veterans since their history books said little.

At counseling, I discovered that although war was the most recognized example causing PTSD, there were many others. The common denominator, though, regardless of how they got it, seemed that they just couldn't stop remembering.

Taking the advice of my counselor, I told one of my stories about the war during dinner. My mom got a funny look on her face and left the table. She returned with the C-ration box containing the war trophies I had sent home nearly twenty years earlier.

"Here's something you sent for us to keep. Do you remember?" she asked before heading back to the kitchen.

I had a blank look on my face and stared at it briefly, then asked, "Where's it been all these years?" But I did not touch it.

"In the attic," she hollered from the kitchen, "under a bunch of old worn-out luggage."

My dad said he'd seen it there, but it looked like a box of trash to him.

"That's not what it is to me," she said while pointing to the return address.

Then I took a huge step and reached over to open the box lid.

The horrible smell that poured out caused a wave of memories: images of the dark tangled jungle, charred bodies, maggots, and stench.

Too much to consider at once, I slammed the box shut. The images subsided.

Afraid to sleep that night because of what I might dream, I lay in bed with the lights on, finally falling into a poor sleep.

Days later, I retired to my room and, without the lights, stared at the unopened box. I wanted to try opening it again, but out of fright and fear of reliving the pain again, I didn't. At least leaving it closed, I'd avoid those memories, I told myself. I fell off to sleep, realizing one day I'd have to open the box.

Weeks later, I again noticed the box on my desk. Now with the courage to face it, I walked over and opened its top flaps.

Images of the war rushed into my mind like before, as if they were spilling from the box itself. Again it was too much, and I closed the box and dozed off.

After a restless sleep, I sat straight up in bed only to focus on the box.

I realized opening it would be like throwing gasoline on an open fire, like peeling back scabs that covered wounds or touching raw open flesh with a finger, but I climbed out of bed anyway and slowly opened it.

Everything I'd packed in the jungle beside Hill 1064 was still there. Photos, stamps, money, even the small alligator leather-covered book with dirt on the cover.

I removed the little book from the box and placed it on my bedside table, waiting to see if it would cause more flashbacks.

When it did not, I opened it and gazed at the beautiful Vietnamese handwriting on its pages.

Deciding that was enough for one night, I went back to sleep, fully expecting nightmares that never came; yet, two decades after returning from the jungle in Vietnam, memories the box held were still fresh.

One day my mom looked in and saw me thumbing the pages of the small, alligator leather-covered book. Polly was curious what it said.

I snapped, hoping she'd leave me alone, "I don't know; it's all in Vietnamese, Mom."

My mom knew the predicament I was in. No job. No house. No nothing. Not even a decent car, but she always held hope that things for me would change. Yet without me saying, she knew that I thought I was at the bottom of the ocean under a rock. She didn't know how to encourage me, but she made one comment.

"Well, son, if it were me," she said, "I'd get it translated. There might be something inside that could help you change your life for the better, and then you could write a book about it."

I was a truck driver, not a writer. Besides that, I told her there was nothing any enemy guy wrote that interested me. "Forget the book idea."

As I sat looking at papers typed in Vietnamese, she asked questions I didn't have answers for.

"What's his name? How old? Where's he from?"

I scanned the papers. I found what I thought was a name.

"Right there—" I said, holding my index finger at what I thought was a name. Focused intently on where I pointed, Polly spelled out the letters one by one.

N g u y e n V a n N g h i a

We tried and tried to make it come out right, but somehow our mixture of butchering the King's English and south

Texas drawl in proper Vietnamese didn't quite come out right.

Fortunately, we had to make no pronunciation for the photos.

"Did one of them in this picture know this Nguyen Van Nghia?" she wondered.

I also saw a photo of a boy sitting on a mother's lap and convinced myself it must be a picture of the enemy guy as a child. Another with a girl. Probably a sister. Next, a photo, appearing to be of his pretty wife.

As I continued rummaging through everything in the box, I suddenly realized that I was holding the entire life story of an enemy soldier.

Days passed, and I became obsessed with the little fake alligator leather-covered book.

I recalled flashes of hatred and fear that took me to the edge of irrational violence. Road rage anger in the truck. Isolation. Depression.

I read about others who had experienced the same, from soldiers to rape victims. Each might have had their own unique trauma, but all of them shared equally in their suffering and loss of a portion of their previous lives.

For the first time since coming home, I questioned why I went to war. *Were the North Vietnamese my enemy? Should I have learned to kill? Was the anger necessary?*

Too many questions.

Like my mother, I understood the necessity of building anger in a soldier in order for him to stay alive. I understood the necessity of having him so comfortable with the thought of destroying his enemies that he needed to be able to fight without hesitation. I accepted that, and I understood my mother asking if she had lost me when I lost that innocence in Vietnam.

My mom's idea of getting the little book translated was starting to make sense.

I purchased a Vietnamese/English, English/Vietnamese dictionary and began the laborious process of translating the diary.

At one point, I went to a Vietnamese restaurant in Dallas, approached the owner, and showed him the book. The man quietly read to himself, quoting a little every few moments, but he clearly did not want to be bothered with any serious translation of the little book, so I left disappointed.

An advertisement placed in a paper searching for translators brought four responses, but all proved ineffective. One supposed translator never got started on the project, a second never finished.

Finally, I got word that a man named Vinh was interested in helping. He was Vietnamese and liked the idea of translating the small book into English.

Vinh was from South Vietnam and had served in the ARVN (Army of the Republic of Vietnam). He and his family had been the targets of North Vietnamese aggression and, like me, still fought the war.

He was okay with the translation project as long as the writer was from the south, murmuring he might not do the work when he learned the small book was written by a northerner. "This guy enemy, and it hard to read what he write. I hate him. Maybe I don't do for you," he said.

It was the same story several weeks later, but that made me more determined. Vinh had to do the translation. I was desperate. I needed to read the words of my enemy. To justify his death, I needed proof that he was not human, perhaps an animal, as I had come to believe during the fighting. Vinh had to reconsider.

The language was a variation of his own dialect, and the translation would be slightly crude. Still, Vinh thought he could translate the little book, but since the author was an enemy, he didn't really know. Only after learning the author was dead, Vinh agreed to translate, but he'd do it only if his real name was not used in the Vietnamese community.

Vinh was troubled when we met again. He had to explain something. He hated the author of the little book too, saying, "He enemy, he enemy." I nodded that I understood. "But Vinh must tell true," he said. I nodded again. Vinh was sweating bullets by the time he finally started talking, "The man who write...the man who write—"

Just then, I interrupted, "Give it up, man. What are you trying to say?"

"The man who write this is good man," he said.

"What? Have you lost your mind? You call him 'a good man?'" I was outraged, flashing back to the corpses of buddies stuffed in body bags and of the sights and smells making me puke.

"Yes," said Vinh, unable to explain what he had found in the enemy's little book, "there's something else. You have to understand, Mr. Paul, I know and understand my culture, and even though I don't like what I'm about to say, I have to tell you true. Please don't get mad. Okay, okay, you promise?" Vinh insisted.

"Okay," I said. "I promise. What is it?"

Vinh continued, "This man, this man...this man is well respected in his community. He even family man."

My blood pressure was off the chart. A thousand images crossed my mind, but about one thing, I felt positive: Vinh had to be wrong. Either he'd made a huge mistake, or he was lying.

In a sense, Vinh was the enemy too. After all, he was from the same country as the author of the little book. But he was in the United States. Somehow that made him more human. *Still, he's a liar,* I said to myself.

As I got up to leave, Vinh tried to hand me the translation, but I jerked away.

After hesitating a second, however, I grabbed it and stormed out the door, wadding it into a bunch of wrinkled papers as I headed off to my broken-down old car.

The translation wound up on my desk. Covered with seminar brochures, paperback books, and cassette tapes. Forgotten.

One afternoon I tried to understand the reasons why my family, house, property, job, and virtually everything I'd worked so hard for were all gone, why I was at the bottom of the ocean under a rock.

While sitting in the backyard under a tree I used to play on as a young boy, I examined myself, seeking answers on how and why I had transitioned from a productive father to a homeless veteran.

I remembered my dad telling me as a boy that I'd have to work for everything. For the last two decades, I had done exactly that, but now I was in a world of hurt—a world of nothingness. I had faith in God, but why was I back at my boyhood home? Why had I lost everything I'd worked so hard for, and what would become of me?

While feeling angry at God in that moment, I remembered a friend once saying that that was what people do when they're not willing to take ownership for winding up the way they wound up. Hearing that hit me in the gut where it hurt, but I maintained God was to blame.

One afternoon I slipped into an anger fit. I wasn't angry at myself or my parents. Actually, no one was the object of my rage, at least no one earthly when I cut loose and began screaming with raised fist toward heaven, "Why, why, why have you done this to me?"

Before another beat passed, though, I heard from God.

I was where I was supposed to be. As hard as that was to accept, just getting that word was calming. Someone once said everything happens by design, but I didn't really understand what that meant, but if it was true in this instance, I would accept.

Suddenly I noticed that I'd slipped into a new place, not physically, spiritually.

Someone once told me that God must get some people's attention in unconventional ways. Sometimes that means eliminating things they love or have placed before him, things, so to speak, they could see in their horizontal sight path.

In other words, sometimes He has to move their eyes from things they can see horizontally and at the same time re-direct their sight vertically toward heaven so they can see and receive their new life or new understanding.

"Even if it meant losing every last earthly thing?" I asked.

Yes, the voice said, *it will be worth it.*

Still, I had many questions despite being comforted. As I focused on heaven above, I wanted to know where I was to go, what I was to do, and how a man who was broken in many ways, financially, emotionally, and perhaps spiritually, was to accomplish anything.

Just then, my desk called out to me. As I stepped toward it, I did not know what, if anything, was about to happen, nor why, but things for me were about to change—and my concerns would soon melt before my very eyes.

Sitting on top of the desk was a pile of junk mail, cassette tapes, and paperback books I'd ignored for months. Underneath them was a bunch of wadded up and wrinkled papers I'd long since forgotten.

It was Vinh's translation.

NON-EXPECTED ENEMY

The translation was crude like Vinh explained. Not so much a surprise, but while smoothing out the wrinkles, I became intrigued—the writing looked like poetry. After counting the pages and finding a total of twenty-six, I went back for a closer look.

What I saw earlier left me hoping I was in the midst of a very bad dream and that everything happening was only make-believe and that I'd wake up soon. Vinh's translation was either one big fat lie or a huge mistake, I didn't know which. Yet, as I flipped the pages one by one, I'd find out soon enough what Vinh had done.

In several places, I spotted familiar words.

Words like "civilian," "enemy," "country," "wife," "brother," and among others, "uncle." A little further in words like "home," "mother," "dad," and even "soldier."

That was impossible. Enemy soldiers did not, could not even use such words, let alone know their meaning. Besides, those were human words, and only humans knew and understood them.

By now, I was certain I was being scammed and tricked into believing something good about the enemy. The translator was trying to make Vietnamese people look good with poetry. *That's got to be it,* I told myself. It was a test to see if I'd believe the lie that enemies were human.

Even encountering such questions, I continued thumbing the pages until landing on the last page.

At the top of the page, one word—the title of a poem. One word shouldn't cause anyone to blow his top, but this one did. Anger deep inside, boiling over like hot molten lava getting ready to blow, sent me into a frenzy. I bounced from wall to wall and off the ceiling, screaming, "No, no, no, it just isn't true!"

Polly heard it and came running, "What's wrong, what's wrong?" frantically pleading while tapping on my door. Hearing her rat-tat-tat-rat-tat-tat on the door sounded too familiar, like a machine gun in the jungle, so I wasn't about to answer.

I didn't predict that kind of response, but stored inside me and encased in an almost impenetrable barrier, was a difficult disease—hatred.

When I finally opened up, I was in a tangled web, engulfed by memories of war and surrounded by a dark aura. I said nothing. But Polly noticed that I held the wrinkled translation.

"Is that what the man wrote?" she asked, pointing to my hand.

"Yeah, but I haven't finished reading. It's just too much to stomach," I told her. She was surprised to hear that since I'd gone to so much trouble getting the small book translated.

"It's just a lot of lies, Mom. The translator got down here things that are impossible." Thinking she'd be offended like me, I said, "Looks like he wrote poetry, Mom."

She wanted to know what was so offensive. Soldiers on the battlefield were always lonely writing stuff like that, she'd seen it in war movies.

I gazed at her with a look of vengeance. *Didn't she know the enemy was nothing more than a killer? Something subhuman?* I took it that she sided with the enemy instead of me.

"Mom, look," I said, tossing the translation to the floor, "I'm not gonna read it. You should understand," raising my voice almost high enough neighbors could hear, "We were enemies. We fought in the stinking jungle, he'd kill me just as easily as I'd kill him. They were like little animals, rats, rodents living in holes and trees. They'd pop up out of a hole, shoot one of us, then dive underground and out of sight. We hated that. We hated them."

"Besides," I went on, referring to one of the poems that angered me most and again thinking she'd be as revolted as me, "there's one in there titled 'Love.' Love ain't for enemy guys," I screamed, "it's only for us, humans."

Polly was a loving person. She'd always tried to teach her son to be loving too, and she loved me, but she'd never seen this dark side, my angry war side. She had never gone through training. She'd never been in a war, never seen death. She didn't understand. She didn't have to. She understood things about life, love, and family, and she was quick-witted enough to know how to respond to her angry son.

Polly snatched the translation from the floor and, before sitting down, asked me to make coffee. By the time I got back, she had read every poem and loved them.

Long ago, intuition had guided her during dinner the night she suggested I get the little book translated. Her perception had told her that something the little book held was meant for me. After reading it for herself, her perceptions got verified. She'd been right all along. Inside, she found not a subhuman creature or a little animal but a man with an acute awareness of life, family, duty, and country. His writing... profound.

She understood the power behind writing and the power of love.

If only she could become an instrument in God's hands. She decided the words of poetry on the book's tiny pages were large enough and held enough power to help her son conquer hatred beyond anything measurable. She had always had the belief the little diary was heaven-sent. Now her desire was to help the love she read on paper transfer into my heart and move me from darkness to light. From hate to love.

She heard me coming down the hall, but before I came in, she said a quick prayer.

"Seems he had," she said, speaking of the former enemy, "written this in the face of death. It's poetry about his lone-liness, fear, anger, duty, hope, and love for his country. It appears he had a lot of love for friends and love for his family."

Staring me in the eye, she asked, "Isn't that what you had for us, your family, your country, your friends, *love*?" I stood in silence, trying to think of an answer, but before I could say anything, she began reading the one poem that had angered me most, starting out loud with the title.

Love

Love bears no grudge.
It is not a butterfly and flower.
Love endures until old age.
Do not trifle with love, or there will be
sorrow.
Do not rush love
In order to enjoy it.
Handle love with care;
Be compromising.
Close your eyes, forget about everything.

Calm yourself, listen to the world speak.
Love bears no grudge.

She paused a moment… I had never looked at my mother as a trigger mechanism, but that was what she had become. She was triggering me like nothing I'd ever experienced before.

She continued.

Her voice sounded sweet. A pleasurable sound, resonating like an angel whispering in my ear. In the grand scheme of things, she repeated words written by Nguyen Van Nghia, but the voice I heard undoubtedly was God's.

And though a world apart, I heard the message loud and clear. It gave me pause.

In the movies, producers use a computer graphics technique known as "morphing" (short for "metamorphosing") to change screen images from one to another right before your eyes.

That was what happened to the translation. It flashed from poems written on pages to a mirror, and its reflection was the brightest I had ever seen. As I peered in the mirror, there was not an enemy on the battlefield but a face.

My face.

I'd come face to face with the enemy. That meeting was not pleasant and not as I had imagined. The enemy was not from North Vietnam. He did not speak Vietnamese. Did not live there either. The mirror reflected the truth. The enemy was inside me.

For the first time in years, I saw the enemy that had been causing me grief. The real enemy was not as drill sergeants had said. Not as I myself had been convinced.

Instead, the author of the little book had not come to give me war—but love.

To put it mildly, I was as shocked as I'd ever been. I was caught totally and completely off guard and never thought revelations about my former enemy would hit me like a hammer, but they did and stronger than anything I'd ever felt.

A friend of mine once said that all battles are fought on the largest battlefield in the world. I had heard that before, never really understanding and perhaps never really caring, but that was then, and now was now. The battlefield the friend was talking about turned out to be the gray matter between everyone's two ears.

Somewhere before the end of the poem, my mom experienced a flashback of her own about the day the shipping box arrived. Why it came, she didn't know. What it was there for she hadn't a clue, but before she'd finished reading the poem titled "Love," she had the answer. She'd been chosen perhaps in one of the most all-time difficult tasks. She was to shine a light on her son's disease—hatred.

It was her calling, and once she and the little diary had done that, she witnessed a transformation she never realized possible. Her son went from hatred to a man who loved his enemy right before her eyes.

It was clear as day. The little book had waited in the box for an opportunity to come out at the perfect time, her son's time of need. Polly got the reassurance she'd been looking for: that all things happen according to God's perfect timing.

At the end of the poem, I felt a closeness to another human being I'd never felt before—my heart felt a shift as though something had happened.

My mother believed love was the one and only thing the Creator of our world and the universe actually ever created and that it was the glue holding everything together. Without love, everything simply falls apart.

"There's nothing above the level of love," she said. It was the highest power or energy in the universe, and there was nothing it could not overcome.

Listening to her had been calming. I drifted back in time, trying to think of anything that was more painful than when a lie that had been accepted as truth turned out to actually be a lie but couldn't. I had to admit that Vinh had told the truth, but now I suffered the pain of a different nature.

With the realization that enemies were equal to me and more alike than not, new and more complex issues grieved me. It was one thing to kill a subhuman being, perhaps a rodent, a gopher, or a squirrel, but it's an entirely different thing to kill a human.

The first thing I did the next morning was to make an appointment with my counselor at the Veterans Center. I narrated my time in the jungle, how I had captured a little diary while on a reconnaissance mission and how I sent it home in a cardboard box made from a C-ration carton.

The counselor, pleased I was opening up, listened to the story from start to finish.

"You mean this box," pointing to the box in the photo, "the box you sent home loaded with the tiny diary you captured in the jungle was the same box your mom placed in a dark attic for nearly twenty years? Then, when you moved in with your parents, she retrieved it from the attic and gave it to you? Is that what you are saying?" the counselor asked.

"That's exactly what I'm saying," I said. Then I let my counselor in on my experience that, when my mom read me an enemy poem, her voice sounded as if an angel was speaking to me.

"I'm curious," the man asked, "Which one of the enemy poems did your mom read out loud?"

"The one titled 'Love.'"

Hearing that struck a chord with the man. After pausing quietly for a second, he spoke up, "I've heard most of my adult life that God is love."

A reverent man and Vietnam veteran himself, he knew enough about the man sitting in his office to acknowledge something of great consequence had happened inside him, but he didn't really know what.

"There's got to be an explanation," the man said after hearing the details of my C-ration box. "I think it goes like this. There's some kind of connection between the enemy guy's poem called 'Love' and God, since He is love. It could be that's why your mom's voice sounded angelic."

My mind was going haywire, latching on to every word the counselor was saying. "Go on," I said.

"Most people," the man continued, "think God is so small He's only as big as a box. Get this… He was in the poem, in the box, and in the attic through no fault of your own and, this may sound like a play on words, but you had Him in that box. Heck, He probably inspired the poem that was in the diary, in the box, in the attic, and came at you with the voice of an angel."

"I don't really understand your thinking, but speaking in those terms, it sounds like you are correct," I said.

The counselor continued, "They—they being most people—keep Him confined and enclosed until they need Him. That's when they let Him out. But get this. They don't let Him out until they need Him. The rest of the time, they keep Him locked away in some dark, dusty ole attic. Did ya get that, Reed?

"In your case, you had Him in a box, and He waited for nearly two decades for you to realize your need. Then suddenly, when you opened the box, He ambushed you. He got out and all over you. Hey, you got ambushed when you least expected it."

Still trying to piece it all together, I liked how the counselor put it in terms I could understand. *Ambushed, huh?* I had to agree that was how it all appeared.

The man continued, "God is like that. He is so big He will let people put Him in a box just to surprise them once they discover they need Him."

"Now here's something that I'll bet you hadn't thought about," the man said to me. "When you get hold of this, it will totally blow your mind. God knew from the instant you got that diary that you were going to send it home in a box. He was willing to get in a box for you, fully knowing you were going to realize you needed Him at some point. But you had to be stripped of all your earthly possessions so He could get your attention because you were too busy to even slow down.

"He knew ahead of time you were going to need the love that little diary spoke about on its tiny pages to heal, find peace, and help others in their search for peace. You know," the man said, "you should take your mom's advice and write a book about this story."

After listening and thinking over what the man was saying, I chimed in. "Do you really believe God knew all that stuff in advance and let that diary stay in a box in a dark attic for two decades just to help me and possibly others?"

The counselor responded in a way that gave me a lot of hope. "Why, heck yeah, I do."

"I'm going to guarantee you this one thing," the counselor said. "God is bigger than any ole box. A lot bigger. Why do you think your mom told you to get that little diary translated? It's because she knew. Think back to when you were in the jungle searching those backpacks. Did you have any idea that your hatred for the enemy would be reversed by words of love written in a tiny diary?"

I didn't want to admit hating as bad as I had, but the counselor was correct. I hated the enemy and carried that hatred for decades, letting it fester inside me. I even hated non-enemies of Vietnamese descent who had fought on the same side as myself.

But the counselor said, "Once God got out of the box, He did a number on your heart. He used something as simple as a tiny diary to transform you into someone who will never hate again. If that is not a huge God, I don't know what is.

"Besides everything we've spoken of here today, getting rid of hate is a good thing. Hate is an emotional problem, but it has a way of leaking over into our physical bodies and can cause all kinds of sicknesses. I bet you didn't know that, did ya? I'm glad for you, man. Hey, let me run something past you, okay? You don't have to do it, but it's something for you to think about.

"I've been listening to your story and know it fairly well. It seems to me that, based on what you've told me about your mom and what I know about God and how this has all trans-pired...you need to, well, you might think about naming your new book—"

"Hey, I'm not writing any book," I said.

"Yeah, but you will someday. I think I know you well enough to know you'll do exactly as your mom suggested. Right or wrong?" he asked.

"Well, you're probably right, but I don't really know," I said.

"Okay, now that's out of the way, I think you should name your new book *The Healing Box*."

THE JOURNEY HOME

Twenty-five years after the battle of Cherry Hill.

Tay Giang Village, Tien Hai District.

Early one morning, a young man approached a house thought to be the residence of former PAVN soldier Nguyen Van Nghia. He was looking for a man who fought in the American war.

"Ah, hello, is this the residence of Nguyen Van Nghia?" the man asked.

"Yes, it is. Are you looking for me?"

"Yes, please allow me to introduce myself. I'm Luong Thanh Nghi, an officer with the Ministry of Foreign Affairs in Hanoi."

"Oh really, you have a first name close to mine," the man noted, "Nghi instead of Nghia."

They chuckled, then Nguyen Van Nghia learned what caused the visit. "All right," he responded, "I'll help you any way I can."

As the officer removed official-looking papers from his satchel, he said, "I'd like to ask you a few questions. Sir, I mean Mr. Nguyen, this document seems to be yours." He held photocopies of Nghia's identification card in front of him. "See, it appears to be identification papers that have your name, birth date, and place of birth."

"Yes, yes, I can see that," Mr. Nguyen answered, "but what do you need to know?"

"Well," Luong replied, "I'm trying to locate this man, but I need to be sure I have the right person. Is this your identification card, sir?"

Even though already suspicious it was not his, Mr. Nguyen asked for a closer look.

"It's my name all right," he said, causing Luong to perk up, "but the birth date isn't mine."

"This is not you?" Luong asked disappointingly, pondering how he'd come to the wrong house.

"No, it's not me, sir," and as Mr. Nguyen handed the paper back, he commented that the identification card belonged to a man who had a scar on his forehead just above his left eyebrow.

"Do you see a scar on my forehead, sir?"

After glancing, Luong saw there was no scar though the card said one should be.

That meant only one thing. Luong had the wrong Nguyen Van Nghia, and he was sorely discouraged about that, but while contemplating his long trip back to Hanoi, the man he guessed was the right one inquired about the story behind the identification papers.

After Mr. Nguyen heard it belonged to a soldier who lost it during the American war, he immediately remembered there was another man living not far away who had his same name. In fact, Mr. Nguyen said, he had heard that the man fought on the battlefield in the south, in the province of Kontum, but that was twenty-five years ago.

Luong said, "Please, please, can you direct me to this man? Do you know where he lives?"

"I'm not positive," the man said, "but I heard he lives in another district of Tay Giang, near the main part of the village."

After a few questions from locals pushing bicycles full of produce heading to market, Luong learned the address of a wife, their children, and another man named Nguyen Van Nghia.

This was of particular importance to Luong. If he didn't hurry, it would be after midnight before getting home, he was a newlywed, and they had a baby on the way. However, he was told not to return to the office until he'd found this Nguyen Van Nghia. Promotions at the ministry depended on success.

Before Luong discovered he'd gone to the wrong address, his emotions had gone from excitement to disappointment within a few moments. But now that he had a good, solid lead, he was excited again, and it showed.

As he neared the house believed to be the one he'd been looking for in the first place, he noticed the residence had only one room but was fairly modern by Vietnamese standards and had a garden off to one side.

In the garden was a man. He appeared to have difficulty moving around as he picked fruit. When he noticed Luong watching him, he stopped what he was doing to greet the visitor as was Vietnamese custom.

Middle of the day. Sun was up, and it was hot. Most villagers were out working in the rice fields, but here was a man at home.

The slow-going man approached the edge of the garden, where the Foreign Affairs staff officer asked him his name. This time Luong waited to hear the answer before reaching in his satchel.

The way Mr. Nguyen pronounced his full name confirmed the uncle figure image the young officer had read about and highlighted the night before.

"Very well, sir, this copy of an identification card bears your name. I previously located another man in a district nearby with your same name, but it wasn't his birth date."

Nghia was partially blind. Verifying the birth date with the small print was not going to be easy, but he said he'd try.

"Do the best you can, sir...please tell me if this is your birth date."

Nghia lifted the paper to his one good eye, not fully aware his shaking hands would make reading just about impossible.

The birth date was his, but Nghia became speechless.

"What's wrong?" Luong asked, "Is this your identification card?"

But he couldn't answer in a way that gave him credibility. Nghia began wobbling like he'd had too much to drink, and when he was about to fall, Luong steadied him. But the once strong and healthy PAVN soldier was too dumbfounded to answer, and his mind went blank over what the young officer from the ministry in Hanoi showed him. One thing was certain. The young officer had not been where Nghia had been fighting in a deep jungle far from home. Luong had not been wounded as he had. He had not seen death, tragedy, and destruction on a large scale as Nghia, and because of this, his mind went blank.

He had been working in the garden. Quite a therapeutic activity for anyone, but this man was not just anyone. He was a veteran of two wars. He had endured years in the military, serving his country, fighting first the French and then the Americans, and was afraid of nothing or no one. But the mere sight of seeing a copy of his identification card gave him the shakes. His mind went into overload.

After a few minutes of processing the last thirty years in silence, he spoke up. "Yes, it is mine. That is me. Where did you get that?"

"We received the documents from an American and owner of a documentary film company, Mr. Steve Smith. He asked the ministry of foreign affairs to locate your family, and now that I'm certain I have the correct Nguyen Van Nghia, there is something additional I have to tell you.

"There is another American named Mr. Paul Reed. Only, he has requested to meet your family because he believes you died during battle on March 17, 1968, in Kontum."

IT BELONGED TO HER

In the interest of helping others, my counselor at the Veterans Center suggested I introduce the diary to my group.

When I did, a heated argument broke out, the likes of such I'd not seen since leaving a combat zone. The veterans became outraged because of the diary. Once an enemy, always an enemy, they said before rushing out the door, their fists in the air.

Their misconstrued anger mirrored mine before I had gotten the diary translated and been affected by it, but now I wanted others to see what I saw. See the enemy like me. See him as a friend. See him as a good man. But they couldn't.

Danny Kadinga, one of the veterans who left outraged, swearing to never come back, got admitted to the emergency room that night. He'd gone out and gotten drunk and been hit by a drunk driver while pushing his car to a gas station after running out of gas.

At the ER, they learned Danny was not expected to live. When he did, they transferred him to a nursing home where he existed in a comatose state. The counselor and I were the only veterans from the group who visited regularly and the only attendees at his funeral five years later.

The counselor's only goal in bringing up the diary for the veterans was not to cause us more hurt and pain but to help. Yet the result was to put distance between us.

That was not true of Dale Doucet from Louisiana, a man familiar with Vietnamese culture. After listening to the discovery story of Nghia's humanity and how wrong about his nature the former paratrooper had been for so long, he suggested returning the little book to Nghia's wife. Doucet knew Vietnamese traditions and how important it would be to deliver the book to the man's wife. Especially since it contained a lot of poems about her. "With the war long over," he said, "it is again possible for Americans to travel to Vietnam. It will not be difficult to locate the man's wife in Vietnam since families there are not transient like they are in America."

Visiting Vietnam again was not an idea I accepted well, but at least a seed had been planted.

The counselor called. Several local high school history classes were studying Vietnam. They needed someone to speak. I went to all that I could, realizing that the students actually appreciated my jungle stories and noticed emotional pain behind each one. I confided in my counselor that I didn't think talking about the hideous killing we did in Vietnam was helping, but he said to keep going.

I wanted Americans to understand me. I had been trying to explain the war, my actions, and my feelings toward the war when I was in junior college. There were professors there, however, who insulted me and tried to make me guilty for going to Vietnam, but I soon realized they had an agenda against the war, the soldiers who fought it, and even those who started it. "This man—" one teacher said, pointing toward me, "is a good example of how war corrupts a man."

I tried to be truthful, not realizing that someone who had not experienced combat could not understand what I was saying. My dad had an Indian saying, since he was part Cherokee, "Never criticize an Indian until you've walked a mile in his moccasins."

I explained that I had been young and naive, as were most of the soldiers, but that I served this country out of patriotism. It may have turned out we were manipulated by politicians, civilians, and others, as the professors said, but I joined the military to fight for my family and keep my country free.

We could have been pawns in a killing game where the manipulators were an odd group of uninvolved politicians and survivors of the war, to which they were sending more young men who might die. There may have been many things about the war at home and abroad that were not above board but, "The 173rd Airborne grunts took pride in what they did as they served their country well."

Despite the fact that I was one of many, I wondered what possessed me to go along. Some of it was the patriotism of a gung-ho kid of eighteen who knew life only in terms of black and white when the reality was very much gray. Certainly, I believed President Kennedy, who, before his assassination, had escalated troop numbers from eight hundred to twenty-five thousand men in order to contain communism in Vietnam.

Sometimes I risked losing friendships telling what it was really like; I mentioned watching a mother come upon the corpse of her deceased son who had died only seconds earlier. And none of Alpha Company felt any of her grief over a youth who had tried to kill us several hours earlier.

These were not the feelings of the boy who had enlisted in the army. These were not the feelings of the father for whom Silas, his son, was the joy and stability of his life. These were the reactions of a soldier who had learned to put his humanity, compassion, and empathy on hold. He was a soldier first. Everything else came second.

For a while, I existed from day to day, not ever knowing which way or how much. I came to the notion that depression was a way of life. Then my son joined the little league baseball team, and almost everything changed. I attended all his games with the boy's grandfather, who was proud to see his grandson grow and be able to knock in home runs. That alone gave me reason enough to live. At the games, I met some parents of my son's teammates. One thing I was certain to never do was to let them know my background, that I was a Vietnam veteran.

The *Rambo* and *Platoon* movies were out. The producers did a good job of making ordinary people believe that Vietnam veterans were bad. Crazy. I saw no good reason for adding fuel to the fire by letting them in on the fact that I'd served in the 'Nam. So I never let it be known.

Then one day, a more complete and deeper meaning of the tiny diary came into focus. In a certain sense, it had schooled me as if it had been a teacher. It opened my eyes, enabling me to see certain things that before were invisible, like not only the humanity of my enemy but that I'd been so quick to judge. It really bothered me knowing that I'd hated people enough to kill them while never knowing the first thing about them.

Through it, though, I was thankful that I had learned to love myself and others.

If Nghia were only alive, I would want most of all to thank him in person for writing the poem titled "Love" and tell of my gratefulness of how it had broken hatred's stronghold on my life.

Everything Dale Doucet said earlier made sense about traveling to North Vietnam to meet the dead officer's wife. She should be delighted knowing her husband wrote about her in his deepest, darkest moments as he faced death. And

I noted that I probably held the one and only record of that in the whole world.

I was a little nervous about traveling there, but if the diary meant half as much to her as it did to me, setting a goal to make it happen would be worth it.

I didn't know how that could become a reality, but I was sure that everything I'd taken from her husband's backpack—photos, flag, and the tiny diary with beautiful handwriting—belonged with her.

WHEELS DOWN IN HANOI

Steve Smith, a documentary filmmaker from Seattle, caught wind of my desire to return the enemy's diary to the wife of the soldier I may have killed in Kontum. He talked it over with another Seattle filmmaker, Mr. Paul Scoles. Together they agreed the story should be told on film. A phone call was made.

When I answered, Smith wanted to know if I was the guy who had captured a little book, stamps, money, photos, and flags from Kontum.

When he heard "Yes," Steve said he'd be in Dallas three days later and that he wanted to talk about our upcoming trip.

I said, "What upcoming trip?"

"Oh, I guess I'm thinking out loud," he said.

Three days later, Smith showed up on my doorstep with a lot of camera gear. He thought the story would make a great Public Broadcasting Service film.

That was when I stopped him cold. "Wait a minute, wait just one minute. Are you telling me you want me to go back, no, not back, but into North Vietnam where Americans are hated, a place we bombed, and still a lot of resentment exists so you can film me giving these items to the wife of a dead enemy guy?"

"Yes," the cameraman said straight-faced, nodding up and down.

"Well, now, that is something I'll have to consider. I don't really think I'm up to that. After all, the fellows at my Veterans Center were outraged upon learning I'd gone as far as getting the enemy diary translated. How are they going to react if I go on a trip to visit the wife of a guy I may have killed to hand over things I got from his backpack?"

Smith noticed a huge change in my demeanor and backed off. After a pause for cooling off, he brought up the time he had escorted several other Vietnam veterans back a few years earlier and his production of a film, among others, known as *Two Decades and a Wake Up*. The guys he'd taken there were able to "option" their stories to a filmmaker in Hollywood once they'd gotten home. If there was anything that had the ability to change an attitude and bring a guy back into focus, a feature film was key.

During our conversation, Smith revealed that he was a two-tour U.S. Marine himself, so he knew his way around in Vietnam.

My demeanor became more receptive at that point.

As soon as Smith noticed the change in my attitude, he said both he and Scoles concurred that taking the diary to the deceased officer's wife might make a great film, but he needed to know three things in order to continue.

"Number one, were there other identifying documents with the diary? Number two, were you the guy who actually captured the items? And number three, is the North Vietnamese guy you captured the items from deceased?"

Eyeball to eyeball and not a hint of a smile, I said yes to all three.

"Very well," Smith said, "I've got a flight back to Seattle in about three hours. I'll call you and keep you advised of the details and when to start packing."

Smith sent a one-page overview of his planned trip to escort and film a veteran meeting the wife of a deceased PAVN soldier to the Ministry of Foreign Affairs in Hanoi. A young ministry officer named Luong Thanh Nghi read it and presented it to his superior, hoping to get it approved. Since there were no diplomatic relations at that time between the U.S. and Vietnam, a filming project approval would prove to be difficult. Smith needed Hanoi's permission to film the event and also their help in finding the widow and/or her children. The office of foreign affairs agreed the content matter described in the overview was noteworthy and approved the project quickly.

Right away, the agency started searching for the family. I had furnished Smith with copies of Nguyen Van Nghia's ID card and promotion to lieutenant orders, which he, in turn, furnished the ministry along with other military papers taken during a battle in Kontum. Smith traveled to Vietnam as soon as he learned they'd found the family and arranged a meeting between the American veteran and the wife of the man who died during the battle.

When Smith returned to Seattle, the only news he had for me was that they had found the family of Lt. Nguyen Van Nghia. Wanting to know exactly what "family" was meant, I inquired, "Was there any mention of him?"

"No," Smith said, "when the Vietnamese mention family, it typically means brothers, sisters, children and aunts and uncles."

But Smith decided to drop a bomb square on.

When he traveled to Dallas to interview me a day prior to our scheduled November 1 trip to Vietnam, he revealed the last thing I ever expected. In the midst of the videotaped interview, Smith quietly said, "There's no other way to tell you this than to just come out and tell you: Nguyen Van Nghia is alive, and he's eager to meet you."

I looked at Smith for a moment, dumbfounded, numb. His words were a big jumble. There'd been close to twenty-five years since that battle where I got the diary, and a lot of water had gone under the bridge. For a few seconds before answering, I flashed to those battle scenes, trying to imagine how the man could have lived.

Then, answering faintly, I said, "Wow, man, that's incredible. He wants to meet me? You're kidding... Some heavy stuff."

The realization that I had love in my heart for the man I once hated all because of a tiny diary was starting to sink in. Suddenly it hit me. My head fell, and tears began streaming down my cheeks.

The emotions were overwhelming. Nguyen Van Nghia was the man I had once hunted in the jungles of Vietnam. He was a man I never knew yet would have killed without hesitation. Such was the power of a preconceived notion. The enemy was different. He was not human, and his life was of no consequence. Or so we thought.

But that all changed.

After my mom brought the box of items from the attic, Nguyen Van Nghia had become my best friend and constant companion. A photograph stayed on my desk. I thought it was Nguyen Van Nghia...but it turned out to be Nghia's friend.

I had read and reread the translation of the diary many times, especially Nghia's poem titled "Love," and always found something new or a different way to think about it in my heart. I had clung to the artifacts as a lifeline to the humanity I once thought the war had taken from me. When I finally got up the courage to return the items to people I knew deserved them more than me, I tried to imagine their reactions to a man whose unit had taken the lives of many Vietnamese, perhaps some of their relatives.

At least now, there was one less death on my conscience. One less victim of a cold-blooded teenager who had gone from killing-to-live to living-to-kill.

The enemy whose blood I had not shed was the same enemy who had restored the peace of my soul.

Always, my love, I miss your rosy cheeks;
Your boat has docked inside me forever.
Do you remember the quiet evenings?
The sunset reflecting on the water,
The wind tossing your hair?
The breaking waves laugh in time;
Perhaps the water can measure time.
Please keep track of our memories.
We said goodbye, now we are apart.
The boat has taken my girl home.
That evening my heart writhed in pain.
I love, I suffer.
Her boat still parts the evening waters.
Darling, forget me not.
Be happy during your spring years.
Be sad no longer, lest my heart irreparably
break.
Always remember our promises
To be faithful and forever in love.
Our love is truly wondrous;
Our hair will turn gray together.
You smile, your lips blossom with
Hope for tomorrow.
Today, on the border, I take in the horizon,

Believing tomorrow will come.

—A poem by Lt. Nghia

I, Steve Smith, Phil Sturholm, Mike James, and soundman Mark Waszkiewicz of the film crew circled Noi Bai Airport, a few kilometers north of Hanoi. As the Thai Airlines plane came closer and closer to the runway, we felt the wheels drop. We were close enough now to see reminders of the not too distant war all around the runway, huge B-52 bomb craters.

Some were full of water and huge enough to be swimming pools. Hanoi was the wartime city of my nightmares. The capital of the enemy territory I had once fought so fiercely. I had learned to despise the city and the people in it without ever having seen it. Now I was there, and anger inside me began to well up once again.

As the plane touched down on the Noi Bai airport tarmac and taxied to the gate, I noticed military equipment in every direction. Russian MIG jet fighters. A radar unit and a building with some tall antennas I knew to be a communication center. These were probably targets during the war, and for an instant, I thought that I had infiltrated to do just that.

For an instant, the communication equipment sent me over the wall. *Hanoi Hannah* had been the propaganda tool of the Voice of Vietnam radio broadcast aimed primarily at the Americans down south. The antennas brought her to mind. She was their World War II equivalent of *Tokyo Rose*—a beautiful and comforting voice sending subtle messages meant to demoralize us. She'd talk about how we were losing the war, "Jody," the make-believe character back home, and the way their girlfriends were cheating on them with him. Strangely, there was a lot about Jody that turned out to be true.

Hanoi Hannah ironically used the same approach as our Advanced Individual Training drill instructor, "Jody" was real. What Hannah did not realize was that Americans had coupled the concept of "Jody" with anger towards Mr. Charles. I and others would listen to her, sometimes predicting our deaths on certain dates and, after a good laugh, resolve to fight harder, more viciously, kill more of them.

The plane rolled to a stop. Smith, Sturholm, and the film crew were calm and exited the plane. Only I stayed behind. I was having a problem getting off the plane. I looked out the windows. First right and then left. I pretended to be a tourist.

Unlike my first time, when I had jammed the exit and tried to flee, I sat trembling in my seat. I knew who I was—Paul Reed, civilian, Dallas, Texas, long-distance trucker, father of Silas, former husband. I also fretted that such an identity was only mine to keep as long as I stayed on the airplane.

The cabin was my safe haven, my link with the present. Stepping off the plane was like living my past all over. It was a past I remembered with horror. It was a past that I visited almost every night, in my nightmares. It was a past I wanted to bury. It was just the other side of the exit, but I wasn't budging.

Finally, I was the only one on the plane. I knew what I had to do. I had to rise. I had to get up and grab my travel bags and camera, had to walk down the aisle and down the steps. But I remained seated as if it were all a bad dream only to realize it was not when a flight attendant touched me on the shoulder and said I'd have to leave.

Outside, the day was hot. The sun was bright. The sky was clear. Twenty-five years earlier, mortars traversed the runway only clicks away. I recalled the enemy still fought and celebrated the Tet Offensive. This time, despite the presence of the military equipment, there were no sounds of battle. No RPGs. No small arms. No rockets or grenades. There was no cordite smell. No stench of rotting flesh. No pungent odors of sauce made from rotting fish heads lingering in the wind like before. Not even the familiar cracking sound of AK-47s.

MY HUSBAND'S HANDWRITING

Luong Thanh Nghi continued, "Quite frankly, we informed Mr. Smith that we did not have information that you survived the war. That's the reason we have come here. To discover the truth."

"That's the same thing the army told my wife back in 1968," Nghia told the young officer, trying to make sense of what he was hearing.

Nghia hadn't a clue who these Americans, Steve Smith and Paul Reed, were, but after a long and serious look at the papers, he was convinced they were his.

Images on the papers were photocopies of his little book that was lost in Kontum. There were pages and pages of poetry he'd written while walking south on the Truong Son range and during some of his darkest moments on the battlefield.

Viewing poetry he hadn't seen in years brought the war he'd tried to forget into focus. In fact, after reading a few lines, the thought of the little book returning to them after all this time would be miraculous. "But how can this be?" he asked.

That was when Luong came back around to Mr. Smith. "As I was saying earlier, the Ministry of Foreign Affairs was contacted by American Steve Smith regarding a film project.

He has provided us with the proposal for a film that will be made for American TV, and the ministry has agreed to let him film. You understand that our two countries, America and Vietnam, do not have diplomatic relations at this time. Because of that, this project was very difficult to get approved, but the subject matter of the film made it possible. That's why I have come to you today to tell you of this good news that the American will be returning everything he collected from your backpack during the war."

"The subject matter of the film, what will it be?" Nghia asked.

"Good question; I'm glad you asked. Mr. Smith and his film crew will be escorting and filming the other American I mentioned earlier, Mr. Paul Reed, as he not only meets your wife face to face but also as he returns to her your lost possessions. Please remember, Mr. Reed believes you died during the battle in Kontum, and Mr. Smith has accepted his belief as truth, but if you are found alive, that will mean a very big surprise, one they never thought possible. Mr. Smith has plans to escort Mr. Reed to the battlefield where you two first met in battle, and that's part of the film, but I can tell you now that once they find out you are alive, they will ask you to go to Kontum with them."

Nghia was speechless.

In addition to the fright of not only meeting an old enemy but meeting him in person, he had questions on how this would turn out were it on the battlefield.

He had many buddies who were wounded in the south. How would they look upon him meeting a former enemy, and what statement would it make to them?

Suddenly Nghia spoke up. What he heard earlier had taken a while to sink in. "My things the American collected, does that mean my little book too? Is it coming back?"

"To the best of my knowledge," Luong said, "according to Mr. Steve Smith, that is correct."

There were many things going through Nghia's head as Luong continued, "The American, Mr. Paul Reed, will be here to meet you in person in a few months."

As Luong turned to leave, he said, "Don't forget, he believes you died back in 1968, during a mortar attack. Now that we have found you alive, he is in for a big surprise."

Soon after Luong left, a panoramic full-view movie of his time in Kontum came into Nghia's sight, and it wouldn't stop.

He saw himself sitting atop a bunker in Kontum and watching helicopters disgorging the Americans nearby: a radio call said they might be the First Cavalry Division, but it was not, as the ID cards of two they killed showed they were 173rd Airborne.

He saw himself standing near ammo storage as the Americans began firing mortars, one hitting the ammo storage with enough concussion to rip his insides open and nearly taking off his right leg.

The non-stop motion picture continued, he saw his most painful part…him lying on the jungle floor bleeding to death all alone, somehow waking as doctors began the amputation of his leg, him screaming at them, "Where's my backpack, my backpack?" only to learn that his most cherished possession in all the world, the little diary given to him by his wife, taken by the Americans, was gone forever.

Suddenly the film stopped, and he was able to focus on the present day, which left him with one huge question.

Is it possible the little book is actually returning to Vietnam, to him, to them?

The sun was down, and darkness was about to descend on the village when Vu made it home. She climbed the stairs to their front door and began removing her shoes when Nghia called out to her.

He said, "Vu, Vu, do you remember giving me a small book before I went south to fight the Americans?"

On the way to the oven, she laughed and said, "Yes, of course, why?"

"Today, while you worked, an officer from the Ministry of Foreign Affairs paid us, well, me, a visit. He showed me the papers of the inside of that little book. Pages I myself wrote he called 'photocopies'...whatever that is."

She had been facing the oven, but when she heard what he'd just said, she turned to face him.

"What did you tell him?" she asked.

"That's amazing, I said, and the little book has been gone over twenty-five years, that you gave it to me long ago and that it was lost during the war, but I didn't think I'd ever see it again.

"He showed me the complete little book, thoughts, memories, poetry. Oh, so many memories! When I asked where he got my papers and the little book, he told me an American man had them, they've been in America for the past twenty-five years, and they would soon come back to Vietnam, to us."

Vu dismissed her husband's story as a dream. America was a long way from Vietnam, and the little book had been lost forever; no American would come to see them, she said.

Nghia had many dreams since coming home, and they caused the family great turbulence, so she wasn't ready to accept his story, but it was possible, she thought.

Several weeks later, Luong Thanh Nghi showed up again, but this time he was not alone. With him was Steve Smith. He came specifically to meet and interview Nguyen Van Nghia and Vu Thi Gai, his wife.

Now Vu believed her husband's story was not a dream.

After the introduction formalities, Luong translated, "Ah, hello, I'm Steve Smith; it's nice meeting you both, but for now, I only have a few questions for Vu."

Before they got started, Steve told her he must verify the handwriting he believed was written by her husband, then reached in his backpack.

He retrieved a complete photocopy of Nguyen Van Nghia's diary and passed it toward her. After an anxious moment, Steve wanted to know if she recognized the handwriting. She indicated she did.

"Whose handwriting is it?" Steve asked.

"That's my husband's handwriting."

"Okay," Steve said, "next question is more of an affirmation. Please take your time. Can you point out something that would confirm the validity of what you just said, that the handwriting you are holding in your hands is your husband's?"

She flipped through the pages pausing a few times, then—pointing while nodding up and down—she said, "I've shown him the correct grammar many times, but these are his bad habits, here, here, and here."

It was official.

Luong Thanh Nghi had located the actual author of the little book, and Steve breathed a sigh of relief as Vu passed the photocopies back to him.

The filmmaker thanked Luong repeatedly, but the young officer acted like it was nothing. "Finding him was easy," he said, "Vietnamese people generally are born, grow up, work, and die in the same village."

Be that as it may, Steve was still grateful to the young officer from the ministry who found the little book's author. That meant in no uncertain terms, the man Mr. Nguyen Van

Nghia, who sat before them, was in Kontum on March 17, 1968.

The two men had experienced enough excitement for the day and returned to Hanoi.

Over dinner that night, Vu was silent. Nghia was silent too.

That's not to say their minds weren't reflecting on what they had experienced earlier. Getting the visit from the American and the Foreign Affairs officer seemed like a good thing, but Nghia wasn't exactly sure.

The war had been over for twenty-five years, the kids grew up, and they had reached a comfort level on par with most Vietnamese families, but neither he nor she understood why the past wasn't really the past as they had often told themselves. *Why is this happening now? Why are the painful memories of long ago coming back? That was the past; let the past be the past,* Nghia reasoned.

He broke the silence. "Do you remember that little book, Vu?"

"Of course, I remember. I bought it and gave it to you before you went south. You were a poet. You loved to write poetry. That's why you got the book. I told you when you filled its pages with the poetry of me, of us, I would always be by your side. You remember," she said, "as you read them, you could feel me there with you. Husband, besides the part about being by your side, I had a strong belief about the little book, and I told you that. Do you remember?"

"Yes, I do. You said both me and the little book would come back and that we would return to you. But how did you know?"

"Call it a woman's intuition or confidence, but my parents taught me once if I believe in something to stick with it, and I have. I never let go of my belief that you and the little book will return to me," she said. "Nearly twenty-five years ago, the military found me at work. They said they were sorry, but they brought bad news: you died fighting the Americans.

"At first, I started crying because other women in the district had similar visits and, what they were going to say I already knew, but after a moment of crying, I stopped because I remembered my belief and told them you were not dead.

"They looked at me with a strange look on their face after I asked them to show me your body. If they could do that, then I'd believe you were dead, but until then, I keep believing you return, I said to them. They offered nothing more, then left.

"My mother, seeing my suffering and difficulty as a single mother, tried to convince me to forget you and move on. But I still believed you would return to me; it seems like the night I said those things was only yesterday.

"My fellow workers said I should forget you and move on, but I still believed. While American bombs burst near our village, and I and our children squatted in bomb shelters, shaking, scared we would soon die, I still believed. Playing your favorite flute melody every day the sun came up, I believed you'd hear and return.

"Many, no thousands and thousands of PAVN soldiers went south and never returned to families in the north, but I never stopped believing what I had told you to come true.

"Each time, reading newspapers on the enemy in the south, I still believed both you and the small book would return to me. Our hearts are connected," she said to her husband. "We are like two people and only one heart. Separated for a time by our country, yes, but only temporary. I believe our country also reunited us one day.

"Not for a second did I believe you died. I believed one day you'd return, that is why I played the flute every day. I always believed."

And as his mind percolated over the years of how fortunate he was to have her both in his life and as his wife, her love jumped out at him when she said...

"Husband, love brought you home!"

Now love returned the little book.

FIRST GOODWILL
AMBASSADOR

I went through customs. The bureaucrats were young men and women who were barely out of diapers when their fathers were trying to kill my friends and me. If they were the faces of my former enemies, they were a generation removed. Their hearts were not filled with hate. Their hands were not stained with blood. This new generation was nature's way of cleansing the soul of the land in the same manner as when the first flowers once again burst into bloom on what had formerly been the killing fields of Vietnam.

I instinctively glanced at the men on duty. I saw two North Vietnamese, apparently security or officials of some sort, unarmed, smiling. They seemed happy to see me, their body posture relaxed. There were no hidden messages, no danger.

The first Vietnamese who spoke to me introduced himself as Luong Thanh Nghi of the Ministry of Foreign Affairs. Mr. Luong was twenty-nine years old, handsome, spoke excellent English, and would serve as a translator.

A second man, much older, was Nguyen van Luong and he would be my driver and guide. He was a war veteran himself, having been in the war against France, which the Vietnamese won during the battle at Dien Bien Phu. He was proud of his service to his country, proud that he had been honored for heroism. The fact that he had a government job as a guide demonstrated that his country respected and honored him. He showed me a photograph of himself and a friend, both in uniform, that had been taken during their time of service.

"Have you met Mr. Nguyen Van Nghia?" I asked the translator, curious as to what kind of reception I'd receive. "Does he know I'm coming? What kind of person is he? Does he want to meet me?"

Luong smiled and said, "Yes, I've met him. He knows you're coming, and he's expecting you. He's a veteran of the French and American wars. A very nice gentleman."

The comment about the age startled me. I had wrongly assumed that Nghia and I were contemporaries. If the man was older, he might be in his late forties or early fifties, but I had the impression that wasn't what the translator meant. "Is he older than me? How much older?"

"I think he's about sixty-five," Luong said with an inquiring look on his face. I was startled. The photograph I had studied obsessively was that of a much younger man. The idea that I might be a generation removed from his former enemy was not something I had anticipated. It should have made no difference, yet I felt suddenly confused. I produced the photograph that I thought was of Nghia and asked, "You mean, this is not the man I'm coming to see?"

Luong looked at it curiously, as though wondering why I had it at all. "That's right," he replied on the way to their car, "that's not him."

At the car, I received a courteous and humbling expression of respect. As Luong opened the car door, motioning for the visitor from America to get in, he said, "Welcome, Mr. Ambassador."

I responded that I wasn't an ambassador. "Oh, but you are, sir, you are our first American goodwill ambassador since war's end."

I was a truck driver, a homeless one at that, a grunt before, but I understood the awesome responsibility in the title with which I'd just been referred. My only hope now was that I could live up to that responsibility when standing face-to-face with my former enemy.

After a short ride, we arrived at the Government Guest House, 02 Le Thach Street, a hotel in the old district of Hanoi only a short walk from Hoan Kiem Lake. The hotel was a western-style hotel, elegant, where foreign dignitaries and ambassadors stayed. Across the street stood a statue of Ly Thai To. He was the "Great Viet" emperor and founder of the Later Ly Dynasty, reigning from AD 1009 to 1028.

The room was pleasant, quiet, and contained almost flawless indoor plumbing, something of a surprise to me. Only the shower was a problem because it was a hand-held nozzle that barely worked. I had to squat, hold the shower nozzle with one hand, and scrub with the other.

There was a small refrigerator in the room containing several bottles of water and glasses that appeared to be clean. There was a French brand in clear plastic and something unfamiliar that had been boiled and placed in a hard bottle. I settled on the one in the clear plastic.

That night, the film crew and I went to the Piano Restaurant and Bar on Hang Vai Street for dinner. Again, it was more sophisticated than I expected. This was a country where many people, including Nghia, had no indoor plumbing. A single electric outlet was often the only inside power. They had developed the technology, and many people had incomes adequate to enjoy it, but the old ways were still acceptable—plumbing and electricity were not considered essentials after thousands of years without them.

The restaurant specialized in Vietnamese and Chinese cuisines, and I delighted in authentic fried rice. I also wanted to take breakfast back to my room, so I ordered bananas before leaving. I thought I was speaking properly, using both my memory and the Vietnamese/English phrasebook I had purchased. However, instead of what I desired, an elaborate dish of flaming brandy-soaked bananas was presented to me. It reminded me of a birthday party at a Red Lobster when the waiters and waitresses bring out a cake with flaming candles. The film crew looked at each other with amusement.

It was late when we finished our dinner, and the hotel was far enough from the restaurant that we decided to hail a cyclo-driver. This was a type of rickshaw powered by a solo driver. Competition among the men who operated them was fierce, and the effort to hail one brought fifteen drivers instantly vying for business.

The cyclo drivers had the same reckless abandon as New York City taxi drivers. In all of Hanoi, there were only two or three intersections controlled by traffic signals. Collisions were frequent, and rides could be quite wild as the drivers weaved in and out, vying with each other for space on the crowded backstreets of Hanoi. Only the tourists were saved from the constant jostling of vehicles coming too close together.

The drivers rang a handlebar-mounted hand-bell every few feet to alert passersby that the passenger was a foreigner. The bell alerted the people to keep a greater distance. They wanted the tourists to have a more pleasant ride, apparently to assure their return.

There were several peddlers selling their wares along the way. I remembered the vendors in South Vietnam, remembered the way every price was at least double retail so they could either negotiate down and still make a good profit or take advantage of the foreigners. This was no exception, though I did not realize it until I purchased an English/Vietnamese phrasebook. The asking price was two dollars, but I quickly learned that the selling price had always been just one dollar. I bought it, amused that some facts of Vietnam life had never changed.

I felt certain that I would sleep well, but by three o'clock in the morning, I knew that sleep might be impossible. My eyes were open and alert for an ambush. I was not having a flashback to the jungles. I knew that I was in a hotel in Hanoi, I just could not adjust to the fact that the war was over, that a tall American was no longer a target for a bullet, a grenade, or a knife. I wondered if the Viet Cong would sneak up on me.

I moved from bed quietly, the stealth of jungle warfare returning as though it had only been days since my last ambush. I checked for movement, for sound. I brought my senses to life, then crept to the door leading to the balcony of my room. It was still shut and locked, no one having tampered with it.

Slowly, I opened the door and moved on to the balcony. I scanned the darkness, the points from which someone could move in for an attack. All was quiet, peaceful. The only stress came from the humidity that was so thick it was like being enveloped in a rain cloud about to release its moisture.

I stood silently in the shadows, listening for two or three minutes. There was no movement, no enemy, no AKs firing in the distance, and no sound of mortar rounds leaving their tubes. Still, I felt restless, not growing calm for another hour. I wrote in a journal that I had been maintaining, watched a lizard move up the wall, and tried to relax. Eventually, exhaustion took over, and I slept for a couple of hours, awakening to the soft sound of chimes.

I ran to the window, checking the clock as I went. It was 6 a.m., daylight was just beginning, and already people were awake. I saw an aggressive game of badminton being played, and street noises indicated that people were going to and from work. I, too, wanted to be up and, since I could not eat in my room as planned, I went to the hotel restaurant for bananas, papaya, orange juice, and buttered toast.

Steve Smith, along with crew members Phil Sturholm, Mike James, and Mark Waszkiewicz, were already there and had begun eating.

Not long afterward, Luong joined us to discuss the day's activities during our trip to Thai Binh and tell us a little about Nguyen Van Nghia.

When the American War was increasing in intensity, Nghia's wife and children encouraged him to join the army again once they heard over loudspeakers that troops were needed to fight the Americans in the south. The year was 1965, he was thirty-seven years old and a veteran of the French war. Yet they all felt that he had to do something for the nation, even though it might mean never returning.

Nghia's family received a small sum of money when he returned to duty. However, though they planned to spend time together, there was never an opportunity. Sometimes the war was too intense, and Nghia too far from home for him to make a visit. At other times, the area set aside for rest and recreation was not safe: random American patrols created a great danger for anyone attempting to navigate the Truong Son range, and the distance was too great. Nghia frequently wrote letters to his wife, but getting them to her was difficult. During the years he served in the South, only one of his letters made it to her.

The couple had a reversal of the traditional relationship because his wife had to raise crops, make money, and take care of the family in her husband's absence. The situation was not unusual in the American War, though. Many women had their husbands serving in the South. They were forced to live in the same nontraditional way as women who lived in the United States during World War II.

At that time, the women went from being housewives or living with their parents to working in factories and running businesses. They developed an independence that changed their attitudes when the men returned and wanted to resume their traditional social dominance. The same occurred in North Vietnam, though in Nghia's family, he was so respected that his wife and children continued to defer to him even though he sustained such severe war wounds that he could never work the land again.

What I did not realize was that Nghia did not share my emotions about meeting his former enemies, was not still angry. He followed the religious beliefs of the ancients, in which the past—whether the day before or a lifetime ago—was over. It had no meaning. Only the present and the future were significant.

"The moment Nghia left the battlefield," said Nghi, "Mr. Reed, you were not his enemy."

Luong paused before continuing, "The war ended and with it the anger, the hatred and the desire for revenge. Nghia understood that what was appropriate in times of violence was not appropriate in a time of peace. He neither hates nor fears you, Mr. Reed. The shooting had stopped, and, so far as he was concerned, for the twenty years since the war had ended, you, who had once been his enemy, were already his friend."

Of all who sat at the table, only half were veterans, but by the time Luong had finished speaking, everyone was ready to meet the man who'd been unknowingly connected to me by a tiny diary so many years earlier.

The small journal had gone full-circle around the earth and was returning to its rightful owner, not according to a pact made between fellow soldiers in the jungle, not for the sake of fairness, honor, or justness.

Love brought it home!

ONCE AN ENEMY

When we got to the Red River on the way to Mr. Nghia's house, the driver informed us that we had about a forty-five-minute wait. The bridge spanning the river, he said, had been bombed during the war and the only way across was by ferry.

After the ferry got our vehicle and everyone safely to the other side and back on the road, the film crew had a good laugh. Sturholm suggested they should build a new bridge back there, they could name it the "Nguyen Van Nghia and Paul Reed Memorial Bridge." The laughter was good. It broke the tension that was building in me, about where I was and how I'd be received.

The trip to Thai Binh City, the capital of Thai Binh Province where Nghia lived, was a three-and-a-half-hour drive from Hanoi.

I was scared as we approached Nghia's home. It was in what looked like an alleyway with two-story buildings on the right and one-story buildings on the left. The right side was for commerce, the lower floor was used for whatever business the owner was in, and the upper floor was reserved for living quarters.

The street-alley was just wide enough for a van. Tall vegetation obscured the view down a smaller pathway, just off the wider street, where the interpreter told the driver to stop. The foliage reminded me of areas where the other men and I used to set up ambushes during the war. My experiences in combat taught me to never use a trail. The reality, in the form of a sniper's bullet, awaited.

"Are you ready?" asked Luong.

I did not know if I was ready or not, but I nodded my head up and down like I was. Several children had gathered: they were silently staring at me, perhaps wondering why there were two cameras following my every move. I wondered if I was really that different. I wondered if they had ever seen an American. I found out later they hadn't.

I wondered privately if I should turn and run, look for a weapon, or simply sneak off. As we took those last few steps, the thought of asking if Nghia had any AK-47s or grenades crossed my mind but got derailed when I suddenly remembered my cordial welcome at Noi Bai Airport.

Nghia was standing in his courtyard as we rounded the corner, dressed in a green shirt and slightly darker green pants; his family lined up close to the house, watching from a distance, almost as frightened as I was.

When the two of us came face to face, Nghia was visibly frightened, hands visibly trembling with fear like a small boy afraid of a monster.

But I was not as shaken. As I flashed back to Kontum the day I flipped the pages of the man's little diary between my thumbs, I realized our first meeting was then, and between then and now, I concluded, I'd gotten to know the man, the poet.

This day had been a long time coming. Two former battlefield enemies who once desired nothing more than to kill one another looked deeply into each other's eyes as Smith, Sturholm, and the sound man, Waszkiewicz, zoomed in, making sure nothing was lost.

I was a big American, much larger than him, my hands capable of engulfing his when suddenly he placed both my hands in his own. He held them the way a father might hold those of a child sitting up in bed, afraid of whatever lurks in the darkness. The older man was at once loving and reassuring, saying more with a touch and a look than I could express in words. I noticed only gentleness and a degree of jitters: Nghia's knees were shaking. I wasn't without nervousness myself and mistakenly addressed Nghia with our translator Luong's given name, Nghi, since they were so similar.

Luong ignored the mistake and simply translated. "How do you do?" I had been thinking about what I would say ever since I knew Nghia was alive, but suddenly I went silent. Everything seemed so awkward until Nghia's reply.

Nghia answered the question posed to him in Vietnamese, which, translated to English, meant, "I'm fine, thank you. Won't you join me for tea?"

Then, taking me by the hand, he gently led me into his house and offered me a place to sit. The front doors and windows were wide open as they usually were, the light comforting.

The invitation to tea was customary, a ritual of politeness. And when we entered the home, small by American standards but quite comfortable for Nghia and his family, there were several people sitting on a rice mat bed at one end of the room. I did not know if they were family members, neighbors, or others who had come to see the American. Certainly, there was more company than normal, for every place to sit was taken—small chairs, the windowsill, even each other's laps. All were smiling. All seemed genuinely glad to see the man who'd come so far to meet one of their own.

Children from the neighborhood peered in through open windows.

The house was a comfortable size, 20 × 20, raised up two steps and clad in a faded yellow stucco. Open shutters would keep out bad weather when closed.

Inside, the walls were decorated with colorful posters, and curtains could be pulled for privacy.

Besides the large bed, there were several chairs, one small table, and one large table. The kitchen was in the corner, diagonal from the bed.

There was running water, yet the family toilet was outside around the corner, reminding me of a farmer's house where I got sick back during the war. Electricity was limited to one five-watt bulb hanging from the ceiling.

Eight teacups on eight saucers had been arranged around the table. The very best china was being used.

Still frightened of the unknown, I hoped to sit on the chair placed closest to the door. I wanted to be able to flee, to leave the house, leave the country. Nghia would have nothing to do with my wishes, though. It was important that I showed deference for Nghia's wife—the woman Nghia loved and to whom so much of his writing was dedicated—and the son who let him retain his pride. Nghia would sit on their guest's left, his wife on the right. He was honoring her, and my fears would have to be ignored in light of that.

The conversation briefly turned to my family. Again, a ritual. I was then supposed to ask about Mr. Nghia's. But, although coached on this ritual, I forgot it when I arrived. Although I failed to ask Nghia about his own family, he ignored the mistake. Such manners seemed of minor consequence given the importance of the moment.

We sat together, hands folded in our respective laps, our bodies tense. There was no anger, no hint of hostility. Rather, it was the nervousness of a blind date, of courtship without knowledge of the other person. Finally, Nghia tried to become more personal.

"I am very moved and very pleased to have you here in my home," said Nghia. "It is quite a long trip to Vietnam. You got my pack during the war. Now you bring it to my home. I am so very happy."

As I spoke, hesitantly at first, then more comfortable about telling the story of mailing the diary home where it sat in an attic for more than twenty years, I glanced at Nghia's wife. She sat on my right, acting as though we were long-time friends. She made me feel at home, having none of the hesitancy, nervousness, or reservations apparent in her husband. Yet she was the one to whom I had once thought I would be delivering the diary. Until only recently, I had believed that she was a widow and the one who had suffered from my actions, the one to whom I could never make amends.

I had thought of myself as the soldier who had robbed her of a husband and father of their children. How it turned out differently, I wasn't sure, but I was happy that Nghia, the poet, hadn't died at my hand and was alive, albeit visibly weak and wounded. In my fantasies of soldiers from the north, they appeared invincible on the battlefield, almost untouchable, with nothing they could not achieve. Yet here was a man who was physically and emotionally shattered, at least as much as myself. The pain we both bore through our experience was the price of war.

Doesn't she know who she's sitting next to? I wondered to myself. *Does she understand I was the enemy Nghia fought in the south?*

Suddenly there was clarity in the moment. As with her husband, the past was always over and must not color the present. Had I killed her husband during the war, the act of returning the diary would have resulted in the same warm, friendly greeting. She was as sensitive to life as her poet/soldier husband. The hate-filled anger that had so thoroughly consumed me during the last decades was not comprehensible to this couple. Just as the war had to be fought as savagely as necessary to win, so the peace had to be lived with enduring gentleness, love, and respect for the former enemy.

Nghia's daughter and two of his three sons, along with a daughter-in-law, son-in-law, and grandchild, were there. The other people were friends. It was an important time for them, a chance to meet an American who had faced their father during one of Vietnam's many wars. They knew who I was, what I had done in the past. But they cared more about who I was today. They were delighted to meet me, to enjoy my company. I was the first American ever to visit their village.

The atmosphere was like being newly married and having dinner at an in-law's house where everyone knows you, likes you and wants you to be comfortable. Mrs. Nghia poured the tea, and I practiced my limited knowledge of the Vietnamese language.

I was in shock. I was having tea with a former PAVN enemy soldier. I had hated this man, hated his family, his beliefs, everything about him, even his country. Yet now I liked—even loved—him, realizing I respected him more than I did many Americans who had failed to do their duty. Nghia had made a stand and fought for what he believed was right. He did not run. It was something I related to and could understand.

The talk and the ritual of the tea continued. Then, before it was time to exchange the old possessions, there was one last rite to perform. Nghia brought out his finest rice liquor.

I didn't drink much anymore. I had gone through many traumas in my life and had found that liquor didn't really agree with me all that much. Yet I knew it would be an insult not to have a drink with the man, so I took a glass.

Nghia filled our teacups, then we toasted each other. Pretending to savor the moment, I sniffed the liquid, realized it was strong, and wondered what to do while watching Nghia take the cup and drink it all. Then, with a hesitant smile, he looked at me. There was no further delay—it was bottoms up.

The strong drink was like a fire slipping down my throat, singeing my nose, the roof of my mouth, my tonsils. Unable to help myself, I coughed twice, then awkwardly smiled and managed to croak, "Excellent." I looked to the side to hide my watering eyes, hoping that if anyone noticed, they'd think they were from emotions and not the liquor.

I told of reading the diary, of coming to realize that Nghia and I were the same. We were two men doing their duty as we understood it, following what we believed in. I explained how touched I was by the writing about Nghia's wife. I said that in the diary, Nghia commented that his sons looked like him and his daughter like his wife. Seeing them in the home, I realized that Nghia had been right, a statement that made the family laugh. I was able to verify what Vinh had said about the author of the diary: Nghia was a good man.

I asked Nghia what he remembered about the war. Very little, Nghia explained. The bombing by the B-52s had affected his memory. His left eye was blinded in the war. His right eye saw little.

Finally, and with some reluctance, I pulled the possessions from an envelope. For twenty-five years, the contents of the pack had been my own. More recently, when the items were rediscovered, they had become foundational in my ability to heal and to help others heal. I was as intimately attached to them as Nghia must have been when living and fighting in South Vietnam. Yet they were captured possessions, not rightfully my own. They were Nghia's.

Letting go of the items was both bitter and sweet.

Bitter because I realized I was giving up something that aided me in my transformation. I'd gone from battlefield warrior to ambassador of peace—perhaps of love. Sweet because Nghia's face lit up with the realization his property had come home. He was amazed his things had traveled all around the world, his index finger going round and round in circles, and after twenty-five years, his things were finally returning to him. I saw the gesture and agreed—that really was something profound.

I pulled out the least important items first, starting with the scissors Nghia carried.

"These are my scissors," Nghia explained, holding them up, showing everyone. "We would use them to cut each other's hair."

The stamps came next. Nghia said that in the five years of fighting, only one of his letters ever made it home.

For the first time, the diary took on an additional importance. One letter in five years to the woman who was raising his four children. She believed in Nghia's love, was faithful to him, had undoubtedly talked intimately for many hours after his return. But the diary would be proof that he had not forgotten her, not forgotten the children, cherished them all. It would reinforce his feelings and thinking during that time apart in a way nothing else could.

The pictures came next, all slightly embarrassing for Nghia but delighting his children and friends. There was a custom among friends to exchange small photographs when leaving. I noted one particularly beautiful young woman who Nghia said was the sister of his friend. It was the only time Mrs. Nghia seemed slightly angered. She looked at the image with tight lips, then looked off. Whatever happened so very long ago was not something she wanted her husband to remember.

The pictures of other pretty girls brought laughter to his children at his obvious discomfort. Nghia tried to explain that pretty girls often gave passing soldiers their photographs. He was as embarrassed as if the girls were still young like their images, although they were probably now grandparents like himself. He had obviously made peace with his enemy but not with the flirtations enjoyed by a lonely soldier meeting a friendly face while trying to survive in enemy territory.

I was beginning to like Nghia too much. In my heart, I knew where I was, what was taking place. But in my anguished thoughts was the idea that this might not be the right man because he couldn't answer some of the questions I had for him regarding Kontum.

I showed him a picture inscribed, "Your loving sister," and Nghia could not identify the face. I was lost, suddenly certain I had been shown to the wrong man, the wrong family. *They want to deceive me, perhaps to hurt me.* I did not know what was taking place and the lack of control scared me.

"That's my southern sister," Nghia finally explained, as though that would clarify everything. What I did not understand was the use of the words "southern sister" in the Vietnamese language and culture. A supportive friend who believed in the same politics, in the goals of the war for unification, would have received this title. This had nothing to do with an intimate relationship, and the meeting together might have been brief, perhaps only a few moments, pictures exchanged as proof of support.

Yet, I was growing uneasy. My paranoia was returning, and I began to seriously wonder if I was with the correct Nguyen Van Nghia. I wondered if the government had made a switch. This was a different man with the same name. This was...

Suddenly, I jumped to my feet, asking Smith to meet me outside.

"What's wrong?" he asked.

I spoke up in a worried voice, "That's not the right Nghia in there."

"Yes, it is," he said. "You don't know it, but we checked him out a long time ago. His wife proved to us the diary was written by her husband, that man inside. We asked her if the writing in the diary was her husband's, she said yes, and our next question was how she knew. 'I always tried to teach him not to make mistakes,' she said. After she showed us where he almost always makes certain grammatical mistakes, we knew he was your man and that he's the one you fought down south in Kontum."

When I went back in, I remembered Nghia's identification card in the pack, the picture taken when Nghia was young; the description on the card told of a number of identifying marks, including a small black scar under the right side of his chin. I brought it out and mentioned the scar, at which a delighted Dien, one of Nghia's sons, jumped up, came to his father, and pointed to the scar underneath his chin, the one on the ID card. I smiled and thought, *This is indeed my man*, satisfied I had the right Nguyen Van Nghia.

Later, when I was calmer, I realized that I had fed my own suspicions by being unrealistic. The war was not so indelibly etched in my memory that I could remember details of the battles in Kontum Province that Nghia could not. Everyone in the United States—soldiers and civilians alike—had access to what were called military "after-action" reports. In fact, shortly before I made the trip, three of my friends, Lewis ("Stony") Stoneking, Bill ("Billy Joe") Jang, and former platoon leader, John B. Doane, sent me letters and details they knew of the battle over Hill 1064.

The photograph I kept on my computer, thought to be Nghia's, turned out to be a Vietnamese friend who died in the war. Mr. Luong had been correct at the airport in Hanoi about the mistake I had made.

At last, there was the diary. I viewed it as the instrument that broke my hatred and set my heart free from a tormented life. As I reached into the envelope, I silently prayed, *God, give me the strength to hand this over.*

Then I spoke aloud, saying, "This small book helped me see you as a good person. Before I read the small book..." My eyes began filling with tears. My face was strained. I spoke slowly, determined that Mr. Luong would hear and understand all my words so that Nghia would know what was in my heart. "I did not like you. You and your unit killed some of my friends."

Upon hearing my words translated to his language, Nghia looked into my face, seeming to have understood long before this day. His face, too, filled with emotion. There was no anger, no shame. He was facing the reality of war that all soldiers must face. There were two sides filled with patriots, friends, men, and women with loved ones and families. Each thought they were right, the other wrong. And each caused what could be unspeakable anguish in the name of honor, duty, country.

As I continued, both cameras zoomed in, and Waszkiewicz, the sound man, moved closer with the microphone.

"And I want you to know that I hated you very severely. But you lost friends, too. And you said in your small book here that you were angry at me, too."

Nghia nodded, smiling. "Are you still angry?"

I began to relax. The emotions of the moment had overwhelmed me, but I knew that I needed to find peace. We were no longer men at war against each other. We were comrades-in-arms who had worn different uniforms, came from different locations and fought for different sides only due to different birth locations.

"Forget the past," said Nghia, as we both smiled. "Now we are friends. I'm grateful it's past. I'm very happy that I lived to see this day." He took my hand in his.

"Do you forgive me and my unit?" I asked.

It was a question I had not expected to ask. From the moment I realized that I would be seeing my old enemy and not the man's widow, I had retained the emotional blinders of the previous two decades.

I had refused to think about the people who had lost loved ones, homes, and a way to earn a living. I had refused to think that the men of North Vietnam paid a much higher price during the war than the men of the United States. After all, most of us, Infantry troops, were homebound after a single year.

I had also refused to see that when two parties are in conflict, there is each person's side, and there is a truth, which often lies somewhere in the middle.

I looked into Nghia's eyes, his emotions again intensely visible on his face. My trip had been fueled by a mix of anger and curiosity of the need to see in person Nghia's humanity and the perceived need to confront. Nghia was the focus for the demons that still haunted my nights, my flashbacks, my work, and my intimate relationships. And now I realized that

I had been wrong in part, that each of us had similar feelings for the other and for similar reasons. And of we two, the older man had come to such an understanding first.

"Yes," Nghia said quickly. He understood. When I grabbed Nghia for a big bear hug, he was a little unprepared, as that is not the culture in Vietnam.

It was an uncomfortable moment for the friends and family members. They shifted in their seats, looking at each other, not understanding. They had not been soldiers. They had not been enemies. Many had not been born until after both the American War and the civil war were over. They had only known a unified Vietnam, the war visible primarily through the scarred bodies and minds of the survivors. But I hugged in my arms the only man who could understand the emotions of that instant. And as we separated, the others knew and understood that we, two enemies, were now two friends.

THEY MIRRORED
ONE ANOTHER

I hadn't really understood the high-value importance of the diary, though I had a fairly accurate idea. To have the poetry, along with the rest of the writing the diary contained returned by an American, actually validated Nghia, his service during the war. No one, including his family, could relate in even the slightest way to the hardships he suffered at that time, yet here was a former enemy who'd traveled a great distance to see him. Suddenly, Nghia was important.

That one act of kindness elevated Nghia, perhaps not for the first time in his life, but for sure over the last twenty-five years, and restored him from that of an assumed head of the household hierarchy to that of the actual head, as he'd been before going off to war.

If I had to guess, Nghia felt a bit elevated in other ways, too, as his military pension doubled.

The next item I pulled from the envelope was the Viet Cong flag taken from Nghia's backpack, commonly known as the NLF or National Liberation Flag. Actually, the flag was one I had sewn in Hanoi, it would serve as a symbol of the real one Captain Davis had safely tucked away in his closet at home, but the meaning was the same. It had been many years since Nghia had seen such a flag. The flag had been used only in the South, and while possession of one is still legal today, displaying it on a flagpole is not. About the time I finished explaining the excitement of capturing Nghia's backpack in the jungle, of opening it and finding the flag, Nghia draped it over his arm and, with a lot of excitement, told everyone the meaning of the colors and star.

"There is red on top, blue on the bottom, and a bright yellow star in the middle," he said while pointing. The red stood for a formerly unified country, the yellow star represented all the "bright, shining people." In Vietnam, blue is a color, which signifies a sad spirit, so blue on the bottom was used to represent the south, separated from them in 1954.

According to Nghia, starting in 1940, Ho Chi Minh designed the national flag. It was solid red, with the yellow star in the middle. During the war, the NLF flag was used to represent sympathetic fighters, who were mainly southern sympathizers who went along with the North's efforts to reunify the nation.

Finally, and now emotionally drained, I gave Smith the nod: it was an indication all of Nghia's items had been returned. Smith gave me thumbs up and a smile, a sign he seemed to be saying, "Good job, I'm proud of you."

Nghia, visibly overcome with emotions like the father of a newborn child, was choked up and could not talk. If his face said anything, it was that he held a deep gratitude inside, a gratitude he'd not experienced before.

When he finally could speak, Luong translated, "Everything you brought back means so much, but because the small book traveled with me to the south on the Truong Son mountain range, it is my most favorite item.

"Along the way, during some of my most inspirational moments, I recorded thoughts of love about my wife, family, and country. I'm not discounting the value of all the other items, please understand, but of all the items you brought, the diary means the most. I was in the underground hospital when I learned you had captured our diversionary camp. I remember that day like it was only yesterday. I was very sad. It seemed that both my wife, who I wrote about in the diary, and the diary itself were gone forever. Now I am moved beyond my ability to express gratitude with words. This is like a miracle. I am *deeply* moved," said Nghia.

I had never thought beyond the return of Nghia's possessions. The joy of the moment was overwhelming, not much different from the exuberance I experienced each time my son knocked a home run for his baseball team.

I did not realize how honored I would feel, coming there and meeting a man I once disrespected, a man I had hated for many years, and who I once believed I killed but now cared for immensely. At that exact moment, I made a vow, promising myself I'd never disrespect any Vietnamese person. Lieutenant Nghia was a man, as human as I was. There was no other explanation for the spirit of oneness that overcame me after my mom read to me Nghia's poem titled "Love."

In a festive mood, Mrs. Nghia invited me to stay for lunch, which I gratefully accepted.

I was seated facing the door to the outside where we'd met only moments earlier. When I glanced toward the door, I was shocked at first at what I saw, although I shouldn't have been.

Hanging just above the door was a nicely framed rendition of Jesus Christ.

Soon the table was covered with fresh vegetables, cooked rice, and bowls of meat.

Nghia took the first step. He put some meat in my bowl and smiled, indicating he wanted me to join in and eat. Savoring the moment, I asked for chopsticks in Vietnamese.

Somehow, Vu Thi Gai understood as she repeated, "*Mot doi dua, cam on yeu,*" and I did get them. She seemed delighted by my efforts. Everyone laughed.

Later I discovered that my request came out wrong. I asked for chopsticks, but the way I pronounced it sounded to her like a very personal word for "love," but Vu's graciousness would not permit her guest to be embarrassed.

What struck me as really poignant, however, was that my former enemy had just offered to feed me in an act of kindness—his kindness was amazing.

Steve said I should give up on trying to talk the language because I'd never get it, or I might say something to someone they take really personal. I agreed.

In many respects, the conversation I had with Nghia that afternoon verified the message I had received from God, the time I became angry at Him back in Dallas. I was to tell this story of reconciliation, forgiveness, and friendship for the rest of my life: that was now clearer than ever. I'd found my purpose in life through, of all people, a former enemy.

Nghia took another peek at the photos and had considerable difficulty seeing them. When asked how he lost sight in one eye and was partially blinded in the other, he told me his eyes were burned by a defoliant the Americans dropped.

It was when he returned to his unit after the near blinding that Nghia and I first encountered each other, during action on Hill 1064, without realizing it and from a distance. PAVN units had their intelligence that operated similarly to the Americans. They knew the distinction between our units and followed us practically everywhere in the jungle. The noise helicopters made was very hard to conceal. They heard them coming and landing. They heard the infantrymen moving toward them in the thick underbrush and jungle.

With a mix of pride and humility, I asked Nghia what he felt when he learned that it was not the First Cavalry Division but the 173rd Airborne, who his unit was fighting.

He said it worried them because the 173rd had a terrible reputation, they were skilled fighters and brought to the battle a lot of artillery and air support. They'd heard of the 173rd's battles earlier in the Cherry Hill cluster of hills or what the Americans called Hill 875 at Dak To.

When Nghia stopped talking, he said, "It was the roughest fighting I'd ever seen."

I thought he'd finished speaking when something came over him. Dropping his gaze to the floor, he calmly mentioned his younger brother dying in Kontum, saying he'd only found out about it nearly a year later. I didn't know what to say, how to comfort my former enemy, but this time, thankfully, instead of bullets and bombs, I could show him kindness. After all, he'd reflected an image of who I was in a deeper reality. I understood we were more alike than not.

Nghia continued, telling how he'd almost died that night during the mortar attack. "The Americans had made it into our complex one night," he said, "startling everyone. We fired, but we could not see our targets. There were a lot of grenades killing several of us. Then, shortly after that, the mortars started coming in. I heard them hit, exploding, they sent tremors all over the mountain top. One of them hit our ammo storage area."

By now, a transparency with an outline had slid perfectly over the lines of my brain map. Before me sat the man who I believed I'd killed—one of the dead in the mass graves when my unit breached the top of Hill 1064.

I remembered the adrenaline rush of the battle, the thrill of knowing how much harm we were inflicting on the enemy. What I had not known, could not have known, was that some of that harm belonged to the man in whose home I would be sitting.

The attack had been a part of the war, and perhaps no one deserves to have to endure war, but it was war.

War was business. It was not personal. Soldiers were there to fight other soldiers. It was not part of an ideal world, but it was necessary to assure unification. The concept did not weaken them as fighting men. It strengthened them as human beings.

Nghia told about the three from his village who joined the army together in 1965. Nghia and his friend Le Thang had both fought the French in 1952–1956. They had worked the fields together. They had worked in construction. They were patriots whose families encouraged them to return to uniform when the unification of their country after the French left was denied.

Le Thang's expertise was in ambushes, and he trained the North Vietnamese fighters in this tactic. He and Nghia, each serving in different units, had been fighting the Americans from the same hill. There came a moment when Le Thang had to take his men through an open area just as the Americans passed over with napalm. Le Thang became a living torch in the midst of that open area, his flesh twisted and melted like a slab of beef tossed onto a too-hot fire. His face and arms were disfigured. His legs lost so much skin that he appeared to have only charred bones to support himself. He lived, but he lived looking like some creature from a horror movie. And still, Nghia did not hate, knowing that my unit was the cause of his friend's anguish.

My thoughts then drifted to the horrors PAVN troops had caused the Americans. I remembered a friend called "Sugar Bear," a U.S. Marine point man who tripped a booby trap and lost both legs before being shipped home. He, too, had lived. And though he was not so disfigured as Le Thang, the fact that both men could be so horribly hurt was a reminder of the brutality of war.

This time it was me who fought back the tears. The enemies should have been friends. Because we mirrored each other, we hurt ourselves as we hurt one another. Victory was in the eye of the beholder, neither side more deserving than the other. To think of all the meeting, talking, and understanding now passing between Nghia and me. All because of a tiny diary.

Me and Nghia holding the diary that brought us together inside Nghia's house.

It was enough talk for both of us. We sat together enjoying each other's company until Smith and his assistant cameraman Phil Sturholm turned their cameras off.

There was a three-and-a-half-hour drive to return to Hanoi, and I would be visiting with Nghia again the next day. Smith said, "It's going to be a long day tomorrow, we'd better get going."

Mrs. Nghia gave me a handful of bananas from their trees, a food I enjoyed very much.

On the way back, as I ate one, I realized the extreme odds against former combat enemies becoming friends; how unfathomable it was through such horror and suffering that friendships like ours could evolve.

The day was productive. I'd made a vow, got answers, and by the day's end, I recognized that I cared a lot about Nguyen Van Nghia. Instead of hate, I discovered that I loved the man.

The most interesting surprise I'd gotten that day, though, was that Nghia's and my connection didn't begin when I first thought—after the diary came out of the C-ration box—it started with the first mortar round I launched against Hill 1064 twenty-five years earlier.

LOVE

As the van turned onto Le Thach Street in Hanoi, on our way to the Government Guest house, I realized what war was all about.

Hanoi could have been Tokyo or Berlin, Rome or Cairo, London or Moscow, Paris, Washington, D.C., or even Richmond, Virginia, the capital of the Confederacy during the United States' Civil War.

Hanoi was the city of the designated enemy, a focus for the hatred that soldiers of the opposing army were encouraged to have as they went into battle.

Soldiers fight more readily if they do not see their enemies like themselves. Seeing the enemy as non-human is made easier by an attitude that does not permit enemies to be fellow humans.

To see the war through the eyes of the man I once wanted to kill caused me to think quite differently about the war and life itself.

And it was all because I had never fully understood there was a time to be born, a time to die, a time to kill, a time to heal, a time to love and hate, and a time for war and a time for peace.

Until the day I met Nghia.

And now I found myself in Hanoi, a city I'd grown to hate, where once I would have killed at the issue of an order.

Suddenly I was seeing men and women, infants, toddlers, and growing children.

Their faces were different. Some mannerisms were different.

Yet I had come to understand that in their hearts, they were mirrors of my own life, of my loves and hopes for the future.

They wanted peace, not war.

They wanted to live without killing.

Yet, they were patriots who would travel wherever their leaders told them to go and do whatever seemed necessary to do. They were just like me.

As I walked the streets of Hanoi on my way to Le Beaulieu Restaurant, I could see and understand that the hate that once encapsulated my heart was gone.

The next day came, and it was time to again go into Nghia's home.

In what had been mostly a conversation between us, two soldiers, I wanted to get Vu Thi Gai's thoughts on her husband's long lost diary returning home, what it meant to her.

She said she had told him before he left to fight that both he and the little diary would return to her.

"Now, my prediction has turned out to be true. I'm glad you have done this, Mr. Reed. And I'm thankful you kept the diary so well preserved," she said.

"In the period 1965 through 1972," she said, "this area was heavily bombed. I was very scared, very frightened." She continued, "When we heard the warning that the Americans were coming, I took the children to the shelter."

I didn't catch her meaning about the warning the Americans were coming, but each time B-52s took off from

Guam headed in the direction of Vietnam, Hanoi got notified. Warnings were announced over huge loudspeakers.

That was when I spoke up, "It must have been the hardest part, not to mention your husband being gone."

When she replied it wasn't, the room fell silent, waiting for what she'd say next.

"It was the death of my husband," she said while wiping tears away.

I was in shock.

"Wait a minute, did I miss something?" I immediately jumped to the conclusion once again that this wasn't the Nguyen Van Nghia I fought in the jungle but the impostor I'd feared the day before. *This was... Her husband was dead? But he was...in the room.* I didn't understand. The scar matched the identification photo. *What the...*

Smith, sure of himself, said, "This is the right Nghia."

She obviously connected with some pain; she wept uncontrollably for a few moments.

No one at that point knew for sure what she would say or when, but all of us were certain that moment was fast approaching.

Finally, she spoke. Luong began translating.

Back in 1968, the military located her in their family rice patty, as well as sent a letter informing her Nghia had been killed in Kontum. Neighbors ran to her as she fell to her knees. They, too, had gotten a similar word and knew the pain. She remembered the day clearly, she told them.

Luong translated as she spoke again. He made eye contact for a moment with each of us before continuing where she left off. She said, "It was only after Nghia showed up on our front doorstep two years later I learned he hadn't died."

"What? You thought your husband was dead for two years, but he wasn't really?" I blurted out.

"Yes, for two whole years, I almost grieved myself to death, thinking he was dead but not really believing. My mother, friends, district farmer wives, almost everyone tried to get me to move on, but I would choose instead to believe he had not died.

"When he hobbled toward our patio, I thought it was his ghost. At first, I wouldn't go near him, but when he kept approaching me, he appeared to be as real and alive as any human could be. I was overjoyed." A smile replaced her tears. "We ran to each other and hugged and hugged."

Smith, who liked to be right, leaned over to me and said, "I told you so."

Apparently, the confusion came around the time Nghia's unit was in combat with mine. The night before my unit captured his diversionary camp and rucksacks, Nghia had been dragged to an underground field hospital, and everyone on Hill 1064 died the next day.

While underground, recovering from serious leg and stomach wounds, he got infected with malaria. It was enough to deal with his devastating wounds, but now with malaria, he was totally useless.

That was the only way one could get released from the war in the south since their service was for the duration. Since everyone in his unit died, it was assumed he died as well because there were no reports that he lived. During this time, Nghia's military unit in Thai Binh was notified that his unit had been eliminated, and a request was made to report his death to the next of kin, his wife.

She faced many emotional difficulties, she told the group.

First, the loss of her husband, a tragedy beyond measure for a couple deeply in love. Second, the shock had to do with the culture of the people. There is a stigma against being over thirty and female in Vietnam. A widow who is thirty or younger is a desirable woman who will often remarry. As a widow over thirty, men seeking wives shunned her.

She would work the fields. She would raise the children. She would lead a difficult existence, the only money coming from what little she could earn until her children were old enough to help. Even then, the rest of her life would be as bleak as the time of separation.

"At night, I felt very sad," said Nghia, speaking of the same time when he was frequently too far from home to be able to help his family. "So far away from home. So empty."

"At night, I would have dreams—nightmares—that he actually died," said Vu Thi Gai.

"Sometimes I would dream about battles," said Nghia. "It was very terrible and very fierce. Why did the Americans come? And why did I have to live like that in the jungle? It was a very hard life."

"Before going south, he was a very strong and handsome man," said Vu Thi Gai. "But after coming back from the battlefield, he was a weak and wounded man. The most important thing to me was that he was alive. When my husband came back home, I was very, very happy to see him again. I thought from then on, my family would be unified. Now husband and wife and children could join together. It's a very warm and good feeling," she said.

Almost as bad as his journey home on the Truong Son mountain range trail, Nghia had nothing to show proving his love for her during the years they spent apart. The poetry he had written about his love for her was gone forever.

Until the day the little diary returned.

BLOOD OF MY BROTHERS

Nguyen Van Nghia and I were scheduled to return to the battlefield where we had first unknowingly encountered each other. It would be the first time either of us had visited the area since the war. It was also the first plane ride ever for Nghia.

Before we left, Nghia wanted to show me how completely he accepted me. He took my hand in his, then began walking through his village, smiling at all his friends, showing off proudly. Nghia was making a statement to everyone that this American was honored, that this American was like a brother to him. The gesture made me uncomfortable, but Luong explained later it was, in the culture in Vietnam, one of honor and friendship.

Wheels down on Pleiku airfield, Nghia uttered a comment giving me a new perspective. He said, "The first time I came here, it took me four months walking on the Truong Son mountain range. Today, only an hour and a half."

The local Kontum People's Committee chairman, when learning of the former combatants' unusual friendship, offered to provide a nine-seat van for the film crew and us to Hill 1064.

Seeing Hill 1064 when the van stopped sent Nghia and me a flood of memories. The ridge where Nghia's bunker was once situated could almost be seen from the logging road where we stood, but most of the tall hardwood trees had all been harvested, along with much of the dense foliage.

The last time I had been here, every second of every hour of every day, the enemy threatened my life. At first, I started to panic, thinking of my lack of weapons. Then I focused on the changes of the present and not the memories of the past.

Yet my instincts warned me not to do that since that's when ambushes happen most of the time—when one least expects them.

At first, when we were moving toward the summit of the hill, I fought the urge to feel for tripwires, then I realized that Nghia probably felt the same way, and I invited him to take a break under a bamboo thicket. By the look on Nghia's face, once we were fully enveloped in the thicket, I noticed he was nervous about something.

Perhaps he was reliving some of his fears; his eyes glanced right then left several times before I asked him, "What was the most frightful thing for you about life in the jungle?"

"Tigers," Nghia replied.

Death was another part of the American grunt's work, loading the corpses in body bags and then on choppers. But PAVN troops did not have the use of choppers to haul their dead off, nor body bags. Burial was immediate, in mass graves, not far from their encampments. "Tigers would sniff out the newly buried dead and eat," a saddened Nghia said.

"These were your buddies you befriended on the Truong Son mountain range trail?" I asked.

"Yes, they were," Nghia replied, consumed by the jungle, lost in the memory.

Near the summit of Hill 1064, we realized we were in the midst of where the greatest violence we had ever known occurred.

With cameras rolling, Luong got Nghia conversational, "We fought and died here. At first, we thought, when we heard the helicopters coming, they were the First Cavalry, but we learned after retrieving two American ID cards, we were up against the 173rd Airborne. We knew of their battles, especially at Dak To in November 1967. They were studied by our military experts in Hanoi. The 173rd had a mighty reputation. When the contact with them ended, everyone in my unit was dead. As I think back about my friends, it is very painful to remember," said Nghia. "Soldier by soldier, they fought the enemy and were killed. All of my friends were killed."

Now, the land was beautiful—the mountains, lush bamboo, and banana trees all freshly painted in shades of green.

I got all choked up. Smith followed me to a tree with the camera, where he interviewed me. I told him, "I can hear the land crying out, 'The blood of your brothers was spilled and cries out.'"

"I once heard that people either run to the source of their pain and suffering, or they run from it," I said. "The principle behind that saying, in most cases, means either choose to begin healing or remain in denial. I'm no longer running from my pain. It's no longer going to control me. I'm going to control it."

As I looked at the ground, I felt as though I could hear the land crying out to me.

Suddenly Nghia spoke, "This spot is where a mortar opened my insides up," raising his shirt and pointing to his stomach.

I cringed in pain. The damages to Nghia's stomach made me recoil at the sight. I remembered the fire mission, sending mortar rounds into Nghia's bunker, ripping apart his position with each explosion.

That both of us had lived was remarkable. That we were able to get together as we had, becoming friends, reconciling with one another, seemed miraculous to me, yet there was one statement we were about to make that needed no words.

In almost perfect harmony, we both saluted one another, then, with our backs to the place of so much hurt, pain, and suffering, grabbed each other's hand and departed down the hill toward the van, symbolizing not only our friendship but that we'd found peace, and flowers once again could bloom on what had formerly been the killing fields of Vietnam.

On our way to the hotel at Pleiku, I felt confirmation that my picking Nghia's backpack to search two and a half decades earlier was the result of the hand of God.

HATE DISINTEGRATES

Nghia's diary contained a number of poems about the Hien Luong Bridge that crosses the Ben Hai River, known as the Demilitarized Zone (DMZ). Roughly the seventeenth parallel, the river divided the North from the South during the war.

Standing at the DMZ, Nghia explained, "At that time, there were two different governments. The South was occupied by foreigners, and in the North, we were taught we should liberate the South.

"I didn't even know what Americans looked like when I heard the loudspeakers requesting troops when they invaded the South," said Nghia.

He explained, while standing at the bridge spanning the river, the first poem in his diary was not his own, but that of a friend who had died in battle. He was Nghia's inspiration to keep fighting and the reason the poem was in the front of the little diary.

By listening to Nghia, I gained a tremendous amount of respect for the man.

Tran Khanh Phoi, the vice-chairman of the Quang Tri People's Committee, came out to meet the two former enemies and escorted us across the bridge.

On the east side of the bridge, there stood a monument, acknowledging April 30, 1975, as the official ending of the war.

The experience reminded me of reading about the American Civil War, where friends and families were divided.

During the day, northern and southern soldiers tried killing one another. Yet sometimes, at night, when all was quiet, the soldiers moved into enemy territory and shared dinner. The vice-chairman said it was the same here.

I commented, "It has relieved me to find out that my former enemy is a lot like myself."

The van took us to Route 9 over toward the Truong Son mountain range to the Truong Son Range National Cemetery. The cemetery is the presumed resting place for over 14,000 of Nghia's fallen countrymen and women. Near the middle of the cemetery is a shrine with an overhead sign, which translates as "The Homeland Takes Note of The Fallen" (*to Quoc Ghi Cong*).

Nguyen Van Nghia and I spent eleven days together.

Both of us relived the violence and were exposed to a Vietnam neither had experienced before.

I had come from Dallas, Texas, a large city in the United States. Nghia came from a village of five thousand people, where everyone knew the sorrows and joys of everyone else.

After eleven days, we had reached our last day together.

In those eleven days, I had wept and sometimes been terrified but had come to love and respect my former enemy enough to call him a comrade in arms.

I had waited for the perfect time to explain to Nghia how much his poems had meant to me and that I was deeply indebted to him for writing them in the little diary.

"Without the poetry," I said, "It's doubtful I'd experience so much change and be able to forgive you and, in turn, receive forgiveness for myself."

Nghia smiled, nodding that he understood. He replied that coming to meet him meant everything in the world. "The best part," he said, "was my little diary came back to me just as my wife had predicted many, many years ago."

The other best part, he said, was who his little diary brought with it when it returned. Our laughter needed no translation.

The next afternoon back in Nghia's village, there was an exchange of presents. Nghia's family, enjoying the way I loved bananas, gave me a quantity to take with me.

Then, as the two of us sat in silence, I pinned my silver paratrooper wings on Nghia's chest. It was the most personal gift I could give Nghia, and it was a heartfelt way of honoring my former enemy, who had become my friend.

Then, standing near the van, I said to Vu Thi Gai and the others, *"Tam biet, hen gap lai, cang som cang tot."* ("Goodbye, see you again, the sooner, the better.") My accent of a combination of Texas drawl and monolithic tone made it come out not quite right, but she understood. When I heard her repeat what I'd tried to say, a smile came on my face. I was the last to get in.

Reed's says goodbye to Nguyen Van Nghia's wife, Vu Thi Gai

After about thirty minutes of bumping along on our three-and-a-half-hour trek towards Hanoi, Luong broke the silence.

It was time for me to know what was said to me as we left. Luong was like that. Sometimes he translated, and sometimes he didn't. I thought this was one of those times, but it wasn't.

"Mr. Reed," Luong said, pausing a moment, "this is what Vu Thi Gai said to me while we were leaving: 'You know, before I…thought…because my husband is often sick, and got wounded, he could not remember very well what happened during the war. But when we received information about his lost pack, and the American named Paul Reed brought back the diary and other items… Our family was very, very happy.'"

Back at Noi Bai Airport and about to board our flight, I remembered getting a report from the archives in Washington, D.C. It gave me the particulars about the battle my unit had with Nghia's: the date, location, and outcome. Once classified but now declassified, the information was titled "Operations Report—Lessons Learned."

I chuckled over that, since reading it, I'd gone through a few lesson learning operations of my own.

"Do you think he will remember me?" I asked Smith.

"I know he will. You've impacted his life in such a way he will never, as long as he lives, forget you."

There was a long pause before Smith continued. "I can see cogs turning in your head, Reed. What's on your mind?"

WELCOME TO AMERICA

Wheels down at Noi Bai. It had been three years since I first landed in Hanoi, now I was back.

On the jet home, after we, two war veterans, first became friends three years earlier, Nguyen Van Nghia's poor sight came up. I told Smith there had to be a way to improve it: maybe it was just a cornea transplant, thinking chemical poisoning had done the damage.

"He's done a lot to open my eyes. I'd like to do something for him along those lines," I said.

Smith said he liked the idea, and they could do a new TV documentary.

I used the advance against royalty I got from the book I first wrote on our friendship to pay for Nguyen Van Nghia's trip to the U.S. Many veterans of the 173d Airborne, including veterans of other units and local community organizations such as Communities Foundation of Texas, donated to the cause.

And now, I was back in Vietnam.

The highway out of Hanoi on the way to Nghia's house hadn't changed much. Farmers on tractors and bicycles with heavy loads still occupied their share of the road, unconcerned about traffic to their rear. Mom-and-pop whatnot stores selling everything from bottled water and canned drinks to cigarettes and souvenirs still sat beside the road, depending upon foot traffic to exist.

Thai Binh City, the capital of Thai Binh Province, appeared as before, but there were more cars.

One huge change: the ferry taking cars and trucks across the Red River was gone. In its place was a new bridge, allowing motorists to maintain highway speeds while crossing the river. Also missing on each side of the highway, where motorists previously waited for the ferry, were merchants who used to sell everything from hanging dog hindquarters to trinkets.

Tay Giang Village, or at least the village where Nghia lived, worked, and played, was only twelve miles from the capital city—easy for the driver to find. His house wasn't. After a few wrong turns, the van finally headed toward people standing on the road: it was Nghia, Vu Thi Gai, and the rest of the family, including some kind neighbors. They were my welcoming committee.

Nghia wasn't in the house, a nervous wreck trembling and wringing his hands waiting on the American like before. No, this time, he was out in the small road beside his house, wearing a brand-new suit and tie and a huge smile. The trip of a lifetime was before him. It was safe to say that none of his fellow villagers had ever dreamed of getting to do what this man was doing.

Nghia was going to America. He'd heard about the place, not really knowing much about it, but now he was going to the home of his former enemy.

Moments before they loaded up in the van, I jokingly asked Nghia if he was ready to eat American food. Nghia, grinning from ear to ear, replied he'd already eaten some. There was a long pause then everyone broke out in laughter as everyone realized he was speaking about the canned C-rations American GIs left behind in foxholes, the stuff none of us actually wanted.

Our group boarded a Thai Airlines flight for Bangkok, where we'd overnight and depart for Texas the following day.

Wheels down, Dallas/Fort Worth Airport, October 1996. Nguyen Van Nghia, Luong Thanh Nghi, and I were met by veterans, TV cameras, and supporters as we disembarked the plane. Over fifteen hours in the air and another three from Los Angeles International Airport, we were exhausted. Hanging in the balance, the wonderful greeting we received made us forget any weariness.

American veterans welcome Nguyen Van Nghia to Dallas.

The greeters had come to welcome a newfound friendship, unlike any they'd ever seen: they were all happy to meet one of their former enemies—this time in a peaceful setting. My contemporaries welcomed Nghia with open arms.

There were others who came to meet the gentleman from Vietnam, not just veterans, young ten-year-old Meredith Boyer held a sign that didn't need a translation.

Written in Vietnamese, it said, "Welcome to America, Mr. Nghia." He confided later that the sign Meredith held was one of the most heart-warming things he'd seen during his entire trip to America.

The cameras and crowd made it the largest photo-op the man from North Vietnam and I had ever attended. Camera shutters were snapping every few seconds.

Nguyen Van Nghia's Dallas, Texas welcome

Soldiers carried cameras in Vietnam, too, capturing our travels to and from our battlefields but none like we experienced in Dallas. This is what Smith warned me about, a project of this nature would garner a lot of attention, and that was circulating through my mind when a newsman stepped up and shoved a microphone in my face.

"Ah, hello, my name is Jim Douglas, with Channel 8 News. I was wondering if you two could spare a few moments?"

"Sure," I said, "but I'm not too good with cameras."

Douglas let me know that they don't bite, and his short interview would be just that—short—but that this was something his newsroom had to have.

After getting a nod of approval, Douglas readied himself and spoke into the mike saying, he'd just finished researching the history of American wars in the 20th century, then paused, appearing to wait for my acknowledgment before going on. Once he got it, Douglas resumed speaking that those wars were World War I, World War II, Korea, and Vietnam. As far as he knew, this was the first and maybe only time a North Vietnamese combatant—an enemy of the United States—traveled to the United States for medical treatment of wounds he received during the war.

It took him a lot of time, he said, doing the research, but of all those wars he found an American or two who brought a former German soldier to the U.S. and an American who had met up with his former enemy in London. The one who traveled to England to meet the Japanese soldier who was his prison guard in a prisoner-of-war camp during World War II, that one was made into a movie, Douglas said. He thought the name of it was *To End All Wars*.

Other than those, he said, he could not find a single instance that was similar to this one—former battlefield enemies of the Vietnam War connecting through a tiny diary. "How do you think your fellow Americans will respond to what you're doing, and how has that tiny dairy actually impacted you?"

I said, "Well, I don't know about all those wars and all that stuff you researched, but this is what I do know. This man—" pointing to Nghia beside me, "I'd be proud to share a fox hole with him any day of the week. He's the kind of guy you could trust with your life. He's got more strength, tenacity, and courage in his little finger than many Americans I personally know. The man has walked over twelve hundred miles round trip through the jungle on the Truong Son mountain range trail or what Americans call the Ho Chi Minh Trail to fight for his country. Nearly dying, losing a leg and his eyesight. How could you not respect that?" I asked.

"As far as how his friendship has impacted me, he wrote a little book that you referred to earlier, you might say…it opened my eyes to a lot of things."

That was when Douglas spoke up, "And now, in a certain sense, you are helping to open his eyes through the eye surgery he's come here for."

"Yeah, that's it," I said. "That's it in a nutshell."

What was missing, protesters. In an earlier conversation, even before their first trip to Vietnam together, Smith let me know not everyone would be amicable to what I was doing. There was still a lot of anger and outright hatred for the former enemies from North Vietnam. It didn't matter, I told Smith, I'd cross that bridge when I got there.

It wasn't long before I got to that bridge Smith heard me mention. I was confronted on various radio talk shows when, at the request of my book publicist, I was asked to be interviewed by a few broadcast radio stations.

I deflected their anger. I'd decided what to tell them long before getting to that place: "This isn't about you, it's about me," I'd say. "It's all about what I have to do to find some healing, find some peace." It was obvious they didn't want to go there. They were not willing to break the mold, happy staying where they were—nursing their own hurt, anger, and hatred. So when they heard the reasoning behind Nghia's trip to the States, that it had nothing to do with them, they dropped their criticism.

The worst possible confrontation came from not an American but a former South Vietnamese soldier. He'd read about the former PAVN soldier landing at the airport in the *Dallas Morning News*. The film crew, I, and others who were escorting Nghia on a tour of the city had the misfortune to stop and eat at a Vietnamese restaurant in Arlington, Texas, which the former ARVN soldier frequented.

He wanted a confrontation. At least he waited until the crew and visitor from North Vietnam got outside and, once there, cut loose on Nghia. He accused Nghia of being a spy. Of course, Nghia, in his laid-back, non-confrontational style, just looked at the man and listened, scratching his head every few moments.

Though I was unable to understand the language, I understood body language, and it told the story of anger. The man danced around like a Bantam rooster getting ready to spur someone, anyone, actually. I was embarrassed for Nghia but didn't know how to call the verbal assault off, so I stayed silent, ready to protect my friend should that need actually arise. It became clear at that moment, the anger the South Vietnamese community had toward the North had not dissipated. It wasn't just the Americans who hated North Vietnam: there were plenty of southerners from Vietnam living in America who hated them as well.

But, thankfully, the man from South Vietnam never got physical. It turned out the man, himself a veteran of the war, was a South Vietnamese community leader and published a newspaper. He was the type of figurehead that translator Vinh, requesting his name not be mentioned in translating Nghia's diary, wanted to distance himself from.

Next up was Nghia's eye doctor appointment. Nghia learned that damage to his eyes was not due to chemical poisoning but more similar to wounds received from concussion; in other words, his wounds were similar to those caused by being too close to explosions.

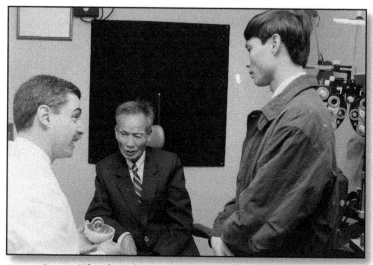

Luong Thanh Nghi (R) and Dr. Bob Pansick (L) discuss Nghia's eye examination while Nghia looks on.

I said, "You mean like if he were too close to a bomb blast?" The doctor nodded his head up and down.

A man watched the evening news from the sofa at home. Thrilled at what he saw, he decided to contact the TV station the next morning.

"This is Doctor Van," the voice with a Vietnamese accent said. "I saw an American man on your newscast. There was a Vietnamese man the American brought to the U.S. for medical care. They were enemies, but now they are friends. Can you put me in touch with the man, the American?"

"Reed, is this Paul Reed?" the doctor said into the phone. When he heard yes, he began explaining the reason for his call. He'd seen the story on TV and told me he himself was from Vietnam, a doctor educated in the U.S., actually a cardiologist.

I told the doctor, "We brought him here to try and improve his sight, thought he might have lost it during the war, but we weren't sure. We're going to try and do everything we can to get his sight restored."

The doctor said, "Well, that's along the lines of why I'm calling," about the time I cut him off. I wanted to make sure the pleasant-sounding doctor realized Nghia was from the North. "You do understand that, don't you, sir?" I asked.

Dr. Van said he grew up in the south, in Hue City, but he thought bringing the man to America was good, and he wanted to help. "How so?" I asked him. The part about him being a cardiologist came up again; he was willing to give Nghia a full physical and stress test, completely free, gratis.

I thought about that momentarily, then said I'd like to meet the doctor in person. That way, we could make concrete arrangements since our time with Nghia in America was at a premium. When the offer was explained to Smith, who had allotted a certain amount of time for filming, he agreed that the check-up or physical should be part of the film.

In the meantime, Nghia and I visited the Vietnam Veterans Wall in Washington, D.C., where I pointed to the names I personally knew who died in the Battle of Hill 1064. If Nghia was uncomfortable while viewing the names of over 58,000 Americans who died in the war, he managed to keep that a secret, but I understood.

That was not the case when we approached The Three Soldiers bronze statue nearby. Nghia froze the instant we came within a few feet; there was no doubt their image spoke to him. While he stared, I stepped back and let him have the moment all to himself. I'd heard most of my life that one could not judge a book by looking at its cover, but Nghia's face was one cover I believed I could. I knew for a fact that Nghia had experienced war much more harshly than I had, the reminders of it all were standing directly to his front, and it showed. This time, it wasn't a wall that held him spellbound. It was the images, the visuals. They elicited some deep emotions, they drew on him. As we turned to leave, he said, "They are so real, they look exactly like soldiers I saw in the jungle. War is death. War means death."

Before leaving Washington, we visited the White House and the Vietnamese Embassy that was not open in 1993 when we first met.

Nguyen Van Nghia's visit to Washington, D.C.

Diplomatic relations had not normalized until 1995, at which time an embassy was opened. Their first ambassador's name was Le Van Bang and his assistant's Le Dzung. Both men listened with a lot of excitement as translator Luong explained how the friendship between two former enemies came to pass because of a tiny diary. Ambassador Le Van Bang commented that the two of us had shortened his expected time of duty in America. "Thanks to you, you've made my job easier," he said.

Back in Dallas, Dr. Van had scheduled Nghia for his physical. After a short ride to the doctor's office, Nghia was introduced to an American tradition—paperwork. Translator Luong helped answer a bunch of non-relevant questions since he was not a U.S. citizen. Smith was there too, securing releases from the assistants who would be part of the film. Smith also had to obtain permission to film inside the operating room, which the management of the Medical City of Dallas readily provided. Both assistants working for Dr. Van, also Vietnamese from South Vietnam, agreed to assist the doctor but asked Smith to not use their image in the film.

On the operating table, Nghia had been prepared for an angiography; the doctor made an incision in his right upper thigh to insert a small camera on the end of a thin, flexible tube. The camera would provide a view of Nghia's blood vessels, identifying any cardiac problems. However, after many attempts, Dr. Van could not get the camera inserted: after poking and poking, it would not go inside the vessel where the incision had been made. At that point, a frustrated Dr. Van reached for the X-ray and snapped an image. That way, he could see how best to navigate the vessel. Click...

I was standing beside my friend in the recovery room, letting him sip water through a straw when the doctor showed up with unexpected news.

"What is it?" I wanted to know. "Nghia has a leaking aortic heart valve," the doctor said.

I understood a leaking tire since I was a trucker, but an aortic valve, the doctor needed to explain. The doctor assured Nghia would never die because of high blood pressure, but while he was making the heart valve problem clear, he told about another strange situation. He reported that he had a hard time getting the camera to go in Nghia's blood vessel and that he made an X-ray.

He stated that had he not used the X-ray and seen it for himself, it might never have been established, but what he was saying was true and factual.

"What?" I asked, eager to learn more.

"When I looked at the X-ray," declared Dr. Van, "I could see the problem, how to fix it, and I went back to finish the procedure. Nghia's blood vessel had been cauterized at about the same location I made the original incision," meaning it was blocked. "So I had to make a new incision in the direction of his heart, and once I'd done that, everything worked like clockwork," he said.

By now, I was eating out of his hand. "What are you saying? What did all this mean?"

"The main artery coming from Nghia's heart running down his leg had been cauterized. In other words," Dr. Van continued, "he was probably bleeding to death when doctors had to stop the blood flow to his leg. They did that by cauterizing that artery. Once the blood flow to his leg had been severed, he was going to lose the leg except—"

"Now, wait a minute," I said while remembering Nghia's story about how he got wounded in battle. "You're telling me the main artery in one of his legs got severed, which stopped the blood to his lower leg. That would mean he'd lose that leg, right?"

"No, not at all. I mean, I see the X-ray where his artery got cauterized." He said, "That alone would stop the blood flow."

I interrupted, "But he'd get gangrene and die when the poison spread to the rest of his body, yes, no?"

"Not necessarily so," the doctor cheerfully said.

"Wait a minute," I said, motioning for us to step out of earshot from Nghia. I pointed back inside the room where Nghia laid. "If what you are saying is true, did he grow a new artery?"

"Yes, it was entirely possible given the set of circumstances during combat, high blood pressure, high excitement, and all. Had his body not been able to do that, he would have died in the jungle," the doctor surmised.

My mind was going in circles when I asked again. "You mean the blood flow to his lower leg was totally lost the moment doctors cauterized the artery to stop him from bleeding to death, then mysteriously, a new artery grew back, is that what you are saying?"

"There's nothing mysterious about it," the doctor said, "the human body can grow new arteries under such types of strenuous situations, high blood pressure and all."

But in my mind growing a new artery in the jungle was nothing shy of a miracle. In other words…*providence.*

Just then, the stark reality of what I was hearing jumped all over me. Had Nghia not grown a new artery, he would not have been able to journey six hundred miles back to the north, would not have survived these past twenty-five years, would not be here today, and I would have never gotten to meet the man who turned my life around one hundred and eighty degrees. *Now that's wealth, true wealth,* I thought to myself, *In no uncertain terms, a miracle.*

We visited one of the largest Vietnamese communities in America, in Los Angeles. Nghia commented, "It looks like we're in Vietnam."

One afternoon back in Texas, I welcomed Nghia to my office, a place where I spent a lot of time at the computer. On the wall, among military awards and medals, hung an NLF or Viet Cong flag. The flag, too obvious to overlook, was not Nghia's focus. Instead, the military medals before him in a display case garnered his attention.

"What do they all mean?" he asked while pointing.

"Well, there's a Bronze Star. That was for successful ground operations against enemy forces. Guess the enemy would have been you," I jokingly said to Nghia. "The rifle on the blue background and a wreath, that's a Combat Infantryman Badge. You had to be Infantry and in combat for over forty-five days to earn one of those.

"This one," skipping over the Purple Heart, I said, "is an Air Medal. We got one of those for each twenty-five helicopter combat assaults."

It was clear Nghia didn't understand, but when he saw me pointing to a photo of flying helicopters, he quickly began shaking his head that he understood. In the background of the photo were the hills and valleys so characteristic of Kontum. He pointed and nodded his head up and down. One by one, he learned the meaning of all the medals; the Purple Heart was last. "The army awarded us one of these each time we got wounded." Pointing to a scar on my neck and left shoulder, I told Nghia about getting hit by shrapnel in Binh Dinh Province during a firefight.

Back in Vietnam, when the two of us first met as friends, Nghia briefly said he'd gotten wounded and dragged to the underground hospital but didn't go into details. Now, however, when he lifted his shirt, he didn't have to point. He had a scar that extended across the full width of his abdomen about an inch wide. As we stood by the medals, I took it that Nghia opened the conversational door by showing the scar. Nghia told me he'd prefer to let the past be the past if that were okay, but when tempted with a cup of hot tea, he gave in.

"It was rough, very rough," said Nghia. "We had to contend with extreme heat during the day and cold in the mountains at night. There were all sorts of snakes, tigers, diseases, and dysentery. The sandals made from old tires and inner tubes hurt our feet, so most of the time, we threw them away and walked barefoot."

I recalled we, Americans, nicknamed the footwear the "Ho Chi Minh sandals."

"It was rough and slow-going in some places. Most of the time, we had no medicine. Some of the men contracted malaria. Some got really sick. The disease was one of the leading causes of death for the men who traveled the Truong Son mountain range trail. Under the best of circumstances, the soldiers became ill. The dead were buried by the side of the trail.

"Several of the men deserted. It actually happened," Nghia said. "We heard them screaming as they were being eaten.

"If you survived sickness and malaria, you had to deal with B-52s. We didn't know they were coming until after they'd hit. It was demoralizing.

"Our units traveling the trail had to time our meals based on when the Americans seemed to be flying the least." Nghia said they used extensive camouflage when they rested so they could not be spotted from the air.

"More than two million North Vietnamese hiked the mountain trail, tanks and heavy artillery used in the final attack on Saigon also used the trail. It was a five hundred-mile journey, filled with snakes and many other dangers. Most of the plant life could not be eaten, and there were limits to the supplies that could be carried. Our throats were frequently parched because water was scarce. Often, the water would not be clean, but it was easier to deal with the parasites than to die of thirst."

"A North Vietnamese soldier," he continued, "starting down the trail, well-fed, with adequate clothing and supplies, would take about three and a half to four months for the trip. Day after day, I traversed the trail, up and down, over-under and through, some days progressing several miles, others barely moving a few hundred yards."

"But of your contact with the Americans…" My interest was in what happened after the Battle for Hill 1064.

"During that battle," Nghia recalled, "it was when I got severely wounded, and your unit captured our diversionary camp and got all our rucksacks," he said. "That night, in the mortar attack, I took shrapnel ripping my mid-section and gashing through an artery in my right leg. That night turned out to be my last night in combat.

"With stomach and leg wounds, and partial blindness, no one was there to help me. I had to return with the clothes on my back and make it home through the dark, dingy jungle the best way I knew how. I used my knowledge as a farmer, all the skills I had gained in warfare, in order to survive on the trail.

"I had several recurrences of malaria, forcing me to stop, to live with the chills, the fever, and the other horrors of the affliction. If I managed to reach food and water each day, there was some hope. If I didn't, I never knew if I would recover enough to keep moving or if I would die from starvation and thirst. One time, I almost gave up…it was because of my wife playing her flute I didn't."

I heard his wife, Vu Thi Gai's account of his showing up two years after the army had told her he died back in Thai Binh. But Nghia said as best he could how his thoughts of his wife and children, of the village where he might, at last, know peace, were all that kept him going. When he finally arrived home, he had to hear his wife say, "The army told me you were dead." Not something he wanted to hear.

His return home was both joyful and sad. Nghia's wife had aged prematurely. She was thinner than he remembered, the result of limited food and intensely hard work. Her skin, her hair, her slightly stooped body were all older than her years. Yet love transcended their awareness of how much each had changed, and they rejoiced at being together again. She knew he would never again be able to provide for his family, yet she and their children encouraged him to tell them how to handle the land and the money they earned. He was the honored head of the house, and so they helped him maintain his self-respect, an important issue for an older Vietnamese male and something many of his comrades in arms lost within their families.

His "Trail of Tears" story continued, Nghia said, because his ID card and papers were in an attic in the United States. When he finally did get home, he couldn't prove his identity, and his government denied him any compensation.

Hearing him say that gave me pause.

That same day Dr. Rick Miller, a local dentist friend of mine and also a Vietnam veteran, called and was interested in donating his time and efforts to clean Nghia's teeth and take care of other dental needs. Only a day or two later, Nghia was in the doctor's hot seat, the dental chair. Although it was his first time there, he remarkably had no cavities.

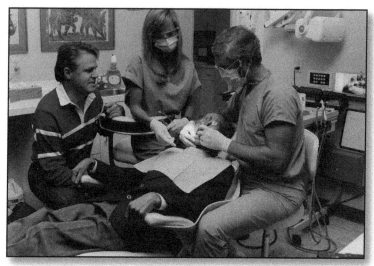

Nghia's first-ever visit to the dentist for a cleaning. Left to right: I, Holly Moshier, Nghia, and Dr. Miller.

When Rick asked what happened to his missing two canine teeth, everyone had a big laugh. It probably wasn't funny at the time, but Nghia was laughing when he told the story, so everyone laughed with him. When I thanked the doctor for his efforts, he said he was both honored and delighted he was called upon.

Rick told me later he was indeed blessed to get to provide dental care to Nghia, that helping him went beyond anything he'd ever experienced, and that helping this man was a *life-changing* event he'd carry with him the rest of his life.

That evening I got a special call from Fort Worth city councilman Jim Lane. He explained he'd seen the two of us on TV and really enjoyed seeing a former soldier helping out his former enemy, especially trying to help improve his vision. He continued, he was a Vietnam veteran himself and was interested in doing something that the man from Vietnam would likely never forget.

"Yes, sir," I said. "What might that be?"

"Well, if you will bring him over to Fort Worth this coming Thursday, we will entertain him and make him feel like he was a genuine born-and-raised-in-Texas individual."

"You're on," I said.

On Thursday, Jim Lane met us on the North Side of Fort Worth, on Exchange Street, near the rodeo arena in the old cattle yards. With him were two Native Americans, Ben Tahmahkera, a Comanche, and Eddie Sanduval, an Apache. A Fort Worth Marshall from the city had also come as part of the welcome crew. They treated Nghia to the steak dinner of his life or at least one he would never forget. I concurred with Jim that it was doubtful Nghia would ever forget the kindness he received on this day.

About time for dinner to finish, Jim Lane stood and said to Nghia that they had a few gifts to commemorate his visit to Fort Worth. First was a ribbon attached to a large key, and as Luong translated, one could see Nghia's face light up as soon as Jim leaned over and placed an honorary "Key to the City" around his neck. He understood the optics alright, but Luong had difficulties translating and pronouncing Jim's words in the drawl known as Texan. As Nghia was handed the citation making him an honorary citizen of the city, J boy from M.L. Leddy's across the street stepped over and placed a beautiful silver Stetson hat on his head. Right then and there, it was clear Nghia was on the ride of his life: he became an official cowboy.

Just then, he began pointing, seemingly across the street toward the rodeo coliseum. "What do you want? What do you want?" Luong asked. Nghia noticed a huge Longhorn steer monument across the street from the White Elephant restaurant as they parked earlier.

"He wants to ride," Luong said. Jim laughed and laughed, then headed to the coliseum, where he personally helped Nghia get on.

If smiles were outward expressions of inward feelings or signs of approval, they were all over Nghia's face as he sat atop that Longhorn. None of them had ever seen a larger smile.

On this day, this former soldier who'd fought against the Americans during the war got to see different people. I remembered Luong, the translator, saying once the war was over, the Americans were no longer Nghia's enemy.

This time the Americans made him feel appreciated, welcome. And he'd gotten to see a part of Texas he would not soon forget.

Nghia receiving the honorary Key to the City of Fort Worth and the genuine Stetson hat presented by J boy of M.L. Leddy western store in Fort Worth, Texas. Left to right: translator Luong Thanh Nghi, Nguyen Van Nghia, J boy & Jim Lane.

I hosted a farewell dinner at a local Vietnamese restaurant in Dallas. Approximately twenty-five guests showed up to bid Nghia goodbye.

Then we boarded the plane for Vietnam. I wanted to see him home.

In Kontum City, twelve miles from Nghia's village of Tien Hai, we were greeted by family members happy to have their journeyer husband, father, and uncle figure home.

Nghia's family homecoming greeting in Thai Binh City. L to R: Standing behind Nguyen Van Nghia translator Luong Thanh Nghi, Nguyen Van Nghia, Nguyen Van Nghia's daughter, and Vu Thi Gai.

Bringing a smile to my face, Vu Thi Gai let it be known she was not sure her husband would come back to Vietnam after going to America. The possibility he'd get snatched up by a beautiful woman was always there, she said, but she was extremely pleased he'd come home, and it showed.

At a local hotel, we said our goodbyes once again, but the sentiment on our faces told a different story. Goodbye didn't really mean goodbye.

Back in Dallas, I sat by myself on a park bench beside a beautiful lake. I realized I was extremely blessed and thankful that God didn't let either of us die with the kind of hatred I'd once had in my heart for the man, the poet—I just hadn't known the real Nghia.

Then there was my mother's curiosity the night she brought the box out of the attic, the first time she laid eyes on the tiny book. She wanted to know what secrets the little book held. Her answer amazed me.

"You should get it translated," she said after hearing me say I didn't know what it said, "There just might be something in there that can help you change your life for the better, and then you could write a book about it."

Suddenly, Nghia's voice…

Love

Love bears no grudge.
It is not a butterfly and flower,
Love endures until old age.
Do not trifle with love, or there will be sorrow.
Do not rush love
In order to enjoy it.
Handle love with care;
Be compromising.
Close your eyes, forget about everything.
Calm yourself, listen to the world speak.
Love bears no grudge.

THE DIARY OF SECOND LIEUTENANT NGUYEN VAN NGHIA

Translated by Rick Murphy and Nguyen Dinh Thich

INTRODUCTION

It is always difficult to translate poetry from one language to another. Word images and sounds which flow artistically in one tongue are likely to seem disjointed in the other. In this case, such problems are compounded by the radically different nature of the grammatical and syntactical structures of Vietnamese and English. *Phong ba bão táp không bằng ngữ pháp Việt Nam* says in Vietnamese, "No storm rages like Vietnamese grammar."

Vietnamese is a fusion of Chinese, Thai, and Mon-Khmer languages. Thus it has words from both tonal (Thai, Chinese) and monotonic (Mon-Khmer) languages. Differences in tone (indicated by diacritical marks above or below the words) can result in two entirely different words being spelled similarly. A careless hand (understandable in combat field conditions) might inadvertently omit one of these marks, resulting in confusion for the reader. Vietnamese words never change in number, gender, person, or tense. But the same word can have different grammatical functions and, depending on its use, many meanings. Meaning is also dependent on word order, which can render confusing the liberties taken by amateur poets. In addition, the system of pronouns (one of the most complicated in the world) is very difficult to render in English. Often, the translators' choice of English pronoun is little more than a matter of opinion.

Because of these difficulties, the reader should be aware that another translator might legitimately offer a quite different translation, even though looking at the same diary.

243

This translation tries for a middle ground between the most literal possible translation (which would conceal its poetic nature) and a freer translation (which would produce refined English poetry and thus may not do justice to simple soldiers who sometimes labored to put what was in their hearts into appropriate words).

There is a long tradition of journal keeping and poetry writing in Vietnam, and it was not at all uncommon for soldiers to carry poetic journals during the war. Due to the fortunes of war, untold thousands of these fell into American hands. A few thousand were turned in to authorities and kept in classified files until well after the war. Microfilm of these (now destroyed) diaries currently resides at the William Joiner Center for the Study of War and Social Consequences at the University of Massachusetts, in Boston. There has even been a volume published containing translations of some poems from these diaries *(Poems from Captured Documents,* by Thanh Nguyen and Bruce Weigl, Amherst: University of Massachusetts Press, 1994).

Lieutenant Nghia's little book was more a resource for his job as a political officer than it was a diary in the traditional sense. He included in it poems written by several different soldiers as well as some of his own. Unfortunately, he cannot now always remember which is which or even what was the significance of the entries of names and dates at the front of the book or the "dedication" at the end.

The following pages contain a reproduction of the complete diary and a translation of each page, even when the significance of what has been written is not clear. Note that the poems often extend for more than one page and that some of them are composed as though written by some other person—a sweetheart from home, a Southerner, etc.

"Memories"
(19)67
(month)
Democratic Republic of Vietnam
Hoang (a man's name)
November 26, 1967
Dang (a man's name)
March 5 to March (?), 1965
nighttime March 29, 1965
July 17, 1965
9:30 April 8, 1965

For seven years, I have stood guard at the seven-span bridge,[1]
So many times, I have paced back and forth.
Life overflows on the Northern shore
And spreads to the high sea.
Oars splash to the beat of the rowing song.
Why does the South so move us?
On the Southern shore of the narrow river
The nights are dark and lifeless.
I feel the crying of the people,
Have met many sweet sisters on the Southern shore.
Their sufferings find me on the other side of the seven-span
    bridge,
Leaving me ever troubled.
Watching the Star Flag billow,
I miss my mother, her warm smile,
In the kitchen tending a fiery stove
On a starry night.
I recall the painful separation
Of a mother from her young son.
For not even a second have I abandoned my post.
I am here for my parents, braving the wind,
A proud soldier of this bridge, of my people.

LITTLE KOREAN BROTHER

Oh, little Korean brother!
Where is your mother?
Where can she be found?
Is there anybody left to ask about
The invaders and war everywhere,
The corpses strewn about?
Snow silently surrounds the villages;
The homes are in ruins and deserted.
Isn't that your mother,
Her white body swinging,
Hair drooping from her skull,
Dangling from the end of a rope?
Isn't that your father,
Hair drooping from his skull,
His gaunt body covered with blood?
No, not so, my little brother!
Your mother is here,
A laborer transporting ammunition.
Here is your mom: she is a nurse.
Your father is here on the battlefield,
Face blackened by gun smoke,
Blocking the enemy's retreat.
Your older brother is here.
Your volunteer brother.
I am glad to be beside you, big brother.

Together with Father, we will slay all of the barbarians
So our motherlands can rebuild.
So our sisters can be happy
And sing in the meadows and rice fields.
We can live in happiness forever.
Today, little Korean brother, the guns are firing.
Tomorrow we will sing a new song.

I STAND HERE

I guard my post this evening
At the end of Ben Hai Bridge.[2]
The steady blue current below
Is like a blood vein joining North to South.
Green rice fields reflect in my badge.
Our nation's flag was handed down to us by our loving
mother.
Each passing moment reminds me that
My parents and native land
Have entrusted this son with the nation's fate.
Standing before the gusts of wind
And the enemy's front-line,
Son, never forget.
Though seven years have passed,
Remember all my advice:
Man your post proudly each evening
For the glory of the motherland.
Though the wind may howl and the rain pour,
Keep looking forward.
Word has come over the loudspeaker;
We are to head South.
My beloved home village fades in the distance.
I miss the harvest season,
I miss the girls of home,
Hair longer than one's outstretched arm.

Now the girls valiantly defend our village.
Hue knows peace and tranquillity;
The Perfume River sings.
My native village knows hunger.
Every night the echoes of Southern gunfire
Tear at my insides.

FROM MY HEART
OF HEARTS

The enemy guns thunder
More madly with each passing moment,
Marking the fall of many of my friends;
They will never know life again.
The motherland weeps for them.
How can we possibly surrender?
We are the proud soldiers of the bridge,
Bearers of the Party's teachings.
We must silence the enemy,
Still them like glassy waters.
I stand here, defending factories and farms.
Day and night, they bustle with activity
So the motherland will be blessed in wartime.
I stand here so my sister can attend school,
So our village can ever greet the new year.
I stand here at the demarcation line,
Looking South, remembering North.
I am divided like the land.

AFFECTION

My rifle firmly in hand,
I cannot leave this land.
I love this land of the bridge's end
Where I have stood guard these seven years.
The pines of Vinh Linh tower upward forever,
I love the rows of folksy houses.
The wind unfurls the Star Flag.
Still, I miss the family hearth.
I picture the road of my native village,
A small lantern shining at each home's gate.
My troops by my side
Bring warmth to my soul.
I wish the country was no longer divided
So we could be together as friends,
Enjoying the pure water of Son Nghe,
The fishing boats of Phu Xa,
Cassava cakes from Ghua Market,
Kim mon sweets imbued with the love of old,
The fish of canoes traversing Chau and Hai Thai.
But the Americans and Diem have partitioned us
Here at the Ben Hai River.
We, the combatants of the bridge's end,
Remain always here
To thwart the enemy's advance.
Our faith is steadfast

Though by now, it's been seven years
Since husbands and wives, fathers and sons
Have seen each other.
I stand here watching the enemy
Forcing civilians to build bunkers.
Many the age of my mother and father labor at gunpoint.
Infants cry out to be breast-fed,
But the mothers must work.
Often I seethe with rage,
Chafing before the division of this nation.

Month after month, I meet enemy soldiers. So how can
I avoid sorrow? We are of one blood, one race. Brother, how
can you be such a traitor! The road you are on is full of blood
and sin.

I CANNOT WAIT IN VAIN

My darling, I can't take this anymore.
I only know my little life.
A diamond reveals its full worth
When shining in the darkness,
Inflaming sweet happiness.
I only want to hear poetry as the sun sets;
I promise I will be loving, faithful.
Our laughter will ring out in every direction.
I only want to watch the autumn sunset,
Your heart beating next to mine.
Our renewed life will arrive on the morning wind,
Once the clouds pass by.
I only want a pleasant autumn.
Love is forever and never forgets.
I will receive your love with open arms,
You are a beautiful flower at age twenty.
I only want your heart to belong to me.
Though we all too briefly shared love,
It gives me a reason to live.
The water flickers as fish jump,
By fives and sevens.
Baby bird sibs soar above the open sea.
I reach out my arms to embrace my country. The surf
    embraces me.
We grew up together, then went our own ways.

One friend fishes these seas night and day;
My memories are like raindrops to the ocean.
Always, my love, I miss your rosy cheeks;
Your boat has docked inside me forever.
Do you remember the quiet evenings?
The sunset reflecting on the water,
The wind tossing your hair?
The breaking waves laugh in time;
Perhaps the water can measure time.
Please keep track of our memories.
We said goodbye, now we are apart.
The boat has taken my girl home.
That evening my heart writhed in pain.
I love, I suffer.
Her boat still parts the evening waters.
Darling, forget me not.
Be happy during your spring years.
Be sad no longer, lest my heart irreparably break.
Always remember our promises
To be faithful and forever in love.
Our love is truly wondrous;
Our hair will turn gray together.
You smile, your lips blossom with
Hope for tomorrow.
Today, on the border, I take in the horizon,
Believing tomorrow will come.

TO MOTHER

Spring[3] is here, your son[4] writes
To wish mother good health, good cheer,
Happy New Year.
The road of hope that would lead your distant son home
Has yet to be paved.
Spring is here; your son yearns for
His mother and native village.
Buds burst to greet the new year;
Love spreads as the blossoms smile.
Spring is here,
Your boy, dear mother, is now a man.
The North sparkles in the new year,
Growing happier as the flowers bloom.
The river below the bridge sings with renewed vigor.
Spring brings food and clothing,
New railways.
The new year stokes the fire of resistance
But leaves your son far away,
For your son clings to his oath.
Spring is here, your son is still here.
Toasting the new year,
Though missing his mother and home.
In the spirit of spring, your son writes this letter
Wishing you happiness, Mother.
My life is the army;

You are married to a soldier.
Lying here, I miss you,
Aching throughout this winter night.
I cannot contain my desire to come home
As my annual ten-day leave draws near.
Sighing, I count the days,
Pining for each next one to come.
The colder the wind, the more I miss you.
Lying here this winter night, who can I tell all this to?
Midwatch, morning watch…
Sleepless nights pass, each watch grows longer.
Thoughts of seeing you still consume me.
Who can stand this war, this kind of life,
I find myself lamenting to the moon.
The more I think about you, the greater my sorrow.
We have missed out on so much.
Friends our age have raised families by now.
I envy them so, husband and wife working side by side each
    day.
They go to sleep, then awaken to the sight of each other.
They are like pairs of white doves.
While we each go our own lonely way.
I dream the resistance has won peace.
I lie next to you, whispering your name.
But you don't answer me in my deep sleep.
Suddenly the rooster crows in morning watch;
We are both alone again.
My head clears, I again painfully realize
It will be many months before I see you again.
I resign myself to endure to the end,
Until the country is reunified.
So I can come home.

A LULLABY

Days, then months pass;
A year is twelve months, each with thirty days.
You sit, numbering the days.
Fully six years have passed since I left.
That day your rosy cheeks were flush with youth.
Their brightness still warms me.
The good old days lapsed into
Ongoing struggle.
At home, you still try to stay busy.
Autumn leaves have fallen six times since I left.
You lean against the door, facing the river, hoping.
You lift your gaze to the rosy clouds overhead.
You look around the yard, hoping
But still, see nothing.
The day I left, I promised
That I would return.
I will keep my promise.
You've lost yourself in tending the rice fields
Since the day I left 'til now.
At home, you are still daily hoping;
Your love is like pink silk.
How can I write all that I think of you?
You are a bird, feathered in lotus petals.
What could be brighter than the glow of us together?
The greatest love is yours.

As I lean against this light pole during midwatch,
I gaze at your picture and return your smile;
So sweet is your expression.
Our love is like the sunrise
Shedding light through rosy clouds.
Missing me, you think up some verse;
With this pen, I will jot it down.
I am awkward; I don't know what to say.
How will I finish this letter,
My heart is bursting.
Though far apart,
The distance does not separate us.
We remain joined
In the spring of our lives.

THE FLUTE

"Last night beside the fire, I stayed up all night.
I made this flute for you, my love.
Until we meet again,
May you see my face each time you play.
Remember our promises to remain forever faithful.
I can see you playing the flute constantly.
Though far apart, you will always be waiting for me."
"My love, you joined the army to serve your country.
Troubled, I yet advised you to defend your native land.
We embrace, oh my dear.
Never embrace another.
Please always remember the flute you gave me.
Remember our promises to remain forever faithful.
Though far apart, I will always be waiting for you.
I stand here in the rice fields at day's end;
Mist clouds the horizon.
My little flute melody
Has been carried off by the wind.
It is for the one I love
Miles and miles away.
The rice shouts with glee in the fields.
The blooming flowers renew my hope.

I sew this shirt with my love
To send to my faraway soldier.
Though far apart,
I will always be waiting for you.
I am always with you."

THE GLAD BLACKSMITH
GIRL OF THINH TRUONG

I look up at the tall furnace
Welding fire brighter than the stars;
I look up at the tall furnace
And see the blacksmith girl
Looking up at the stars.
Daily she returns home, satchel in hand,
To enjoy a pleasant afternoon,
Still doting on her blacksmith mentor.
See her watch the flowers bloom in the morning
So absorbed in the moment;
She must be scolded by Mom.
Brilliant flames well constantly from the depths of her soul.
These find the tall furnace,
Stoking the welding fire to be brighter than the stars
That the blacksmith girl has fixed her eyes on.
She admires the stars as she does the fine welding line
That she so loves.
Day after day, the girl's hands are busy,
For every tomorrow the furnace yields a fresh batch of steel.
She feels happy, watching the country grow stronger,
Flourishing like the morning blooms.
At exam time, the girl is a bouquet of fresh roses.
The tall furnace makes the future as bright
As the countless stars.

RETURNING NORTH TO VISIT HOME

The dirt road leading home is vermilion red,
Ablaze like my soul.
Wind teases the green rice seedlings.
Corn on the hillside sways gently in the breeze.
The banyan tree in front of the coffee shop
Recalls the days when I was young.
The mossy lake with the long bridge
Recalls the evenings spent fishing.
Thatched cottages, bordered by areca and bamboo
Line the banks
Along with jackfruit and banana trees.
The echo of peoples' voices resounds from the empty
     ferryboat
As the pigeons' coo lengthens.
But the charm of the moment is lost
In a homeland that stands divided,
In the heart of a separated lover
Who grieves for his broken country.
One day of love spared for the motherland
Is worth a hundred years remembering
The roof on one's home.

SPRING IS COMING

Spring is coming, see the beautiful landscape.
Spring is coming in sweet-smelling blossoms.
Merry butterflies alight on peach branchlets
Undisturbed by the wind, they hail spring's arrival.
Spring is coming, my heart grows warm,
I think fondly of my young friend far away
In the spring of her life.
She is like the golden moon rising in the sky.
I remember our love; I cannot forget
For a thousand years, it will be etched on my heart.
I still await the reunion
Of a youthful wife and husband, mother and son.
But out of duty to my country
I remain out here, defending the hamlets and villages.
Spring is coming, millions of people are eager to share
Golden sentiments.
Spring is coming, I wish you good health, my love.
Please stay fully true to that which you love.
As you add another choice year to the spring of your life,
Bridle your spirit for the country's sake;
So there will be light for the full moon,
So the lotus blossoms will be filled with a sweetness,
Matched only by our love.
Far from you, my pen is my voice;
Spring is coming, I send my rosy-cheeked lover a kiss.

LOVE

Love bears no grudge.
It is not a butterfly and flower,
Love endures until old age.
Do not trifle with love, or there will be sorrow.
Do not rush love
In order to enjoy it.
Handle love with care;
Be compromising.
Close your eyes, forget about everything.
Calm yourself, listen to the world speak.
Love bears no grudge.
Love is not a quaint flower arrangement.
Don't put on airs; act from the heart.
The price of fleeting joy is an eternal shame,
But in saying so, do not be close-minded.
See yourself as adored by immortals
Lest you age ungracefully,
Finally to decay with the fallen leaves.
May you exalt love.
Be forever faithful; do not trifle with love.
Show the way for the younger generation.
Do not treat romantic love casually,
Lest it consume you. Handle love with care.

TO MY DISTANT LOVER[5]

Today, amid the fresh spring,
We are far apart but still one
In the faith of our youth.
I remember your hearty speech and laughter,
The bright moon rising in the East.
Water running downstream past the wild grass.
The peach's freshness kindles my dreams.
Near you, form truly meets shadow.
During long nights, yearning for you,
I cling to our vows,
Though we cannot live as an ordinary couple.
May your faithfulness never wane.
For a hundred years, meditate on the word "faithfulness."
The letter-lines refresh our memories,
There is so much to remember.
But surely you don't want to dwell on
Our unfinished love, provoking deep bitterness.
I must stop writing for now;
The pen's nib flounders in my tears
My heart can't be stilled…
Together, let us keep our word.
Though the seas may dry up,
May we again laugh together.

SONG TO SEW UNIFORMS BY[6]

Our soldiers are exposed to rain and sun.
The rain chills their insides; the sun burns their skin.
From cloth we fashion uniforms;
Our soldiers are resolved to exterminate the enemy.
My guy fights zealously on the battlefield;
Your gal swears to give her all.
Be quick of hand, brothers and sisters!
Looms whir, gunfire crackles through the green forest.
We fashion our hatred into poems.
Gunfire rhymes with the looms' whir.
We exterminate the enemy to the rhythm.
We sew these uniforms with great care,
For the satisfaction of the liberating soldiers.
Be quick of hand, brothers and sisters!
We fashion uniforms; winter draws near.
Proffering fresh new uniforms to you, liberators,
Gladdens our hearts and brings us fulfillment.
We sew uniforms destined for the battlefields;
Be quick of hand, brothers and sisters!

THE SOUTHERNER'S HOMELAND

I hail from the South,
Land of blue-green coconut forests,
Land of winding rivers,
My homeland is a stranger to hardship.
But after nine years of animosity,
I am determined to carry on the struggle
Until peace and happiness can be heard in
Singing birds returning home,
Golden rice rustling in the paddies,
Boat wakes splashing on glad rivers,
The wind carrying the rower's song.
But how can the South Vietnamese
Under enemy rule
Be so full of song?
Hands covered with our blood,
Their hamlets sadly silent,
Writhing pitifully in the hate.
The people struggle for a single nation;
The future holds unity.
North and South will share the same flag.
Tomorrow we will sing a thousand songs together.
The South is shimmering rice fields,
Abundant blue waters.

Listen to the boats rocking, moored happily on the river.
Troops and civilians live together,
The harvest grows more bountiful
With peace and joy.
For two years, I have fought here in the South;
One day North and South will fight together
To build a bright tomorrow.
As a bird finds her way above the forest,
The days and months will find peace in the South.

Warmly dedicated to Comrade Huu T. East Unit
Dedicated to Comrade Huu on the occasion of
his departure for fulfilling his military duties.
My comrade, carry with you a valiant fighting
spirit. Be deserving of your charge: a pioneer
in the People of Vietnam's Army.
T. East, April 8, 1965
Viet Huong Cooperative
Ward Phang
District of Dien Bien
Lai Chau City

1. The author of the poem (one of Lt. Nghia's friends) is standing guard at the Hien Luong Bridge, which crosses the Ben Hai River, the demarcation line established in 1954 to separate North Vietnam and South Vietnam.
2. The actual name of the bridge is the Hien Luong Bridge. The author of the poem is referring to the Ben Hai River, which the bridge crosses.
3. The arrival of spring coincides with the (lunar) New Year for the Vietnamese.
4. There are no "I" and "you" pronouns in Vietnamese. The translation of this poem seeks to capture that. As it would be non-standard English not to use "I" and "you," they are used throughout the other poems.
5. The author again is taking the role of his wife.
6. This poem is written from the perspective of a girl-friend back home, sewing uniforms for her soldier boyfriend.

THE REST OF THE STORY

Polly Baker, Paul's Mom. Polly reunited Paul Reed with the diary that sat in the attic in a box that became known as *The Healing Box*. Interestingly, she had insight into its power and healing properties long before knowing just how much the little book would impact not only two former combatants but many others and possibly two countries. Without her insight, it's possible the love Nghia had for his wife, family, and country might never have been revealed, and the friendship between her son and Nghia might never have happened. Polly passed in early 2003.

Leo Baker, Reed's Dad. Leo was a petroleum engineer and a quiet man who loved fishing. During a fishing trip with his son, he expressed that he didn't really care what his only son turned out to be or what profession he chose, only that he wanted his son to be the best at whatever that was. Often though, the two men had differences of opinions. However, Leo did confide in his son before passing, that he never realized how badly the war damaged him until he'd witnessed his son's struggles afterward. He marveled that nothing had been able to pull him away from the amazing journey Nghia's tiny diary took him on. It turns out Reed's dad was one of the best friends he ever had, and he truly loved his son. Leo passed in early 2004.

Silas, Reed's Son. His birth was nothing short of a miracle. Doctors claimed he was a girl while still being carried by his mother. But Reed wasn't buying it. He'd prayed for a boy, and as far as he was concerned, that was what he was getting, he said to the doctor. Silas resides near Dallas and is the director of recruiting of a physician staffing firm. He grew up to be a remarkably well-adjusted husband and father. He married a beautiful, charming, and smart young lady, and together they have two fabulous boys, Reed's grandchildren. He was distant during Silas's early childhood, partly because of his trucking career and, to some extent, necessary isolationism due to PTSD. However, his and his son's relationship is closer than ever. It turns out they became best friends like the two in scripture, Paul and Silas.

Loung Thanh Nghi, the translator. Luong progressed from the Ministry of Foreign Affairs to the Vietnamese Ambassador to Australia. As busy as he is, he still takes time to visit, and he sends an occasional email message. The last time Reed was in Luong's office, he paid him a rather nice compliment during his visit to Hanoi, saying he was amazed he was sitting with a celebrity. "No, that can't be true," Reed said. "Oh, but it is. I've seen you on TV at least eight times already," came the reply. Their friendship continues to this day.

Lt. Nguyen Van Nghia. The former PAVN First Lieutenant became a National Treasure and still lives in Thai Binh City, about seventy miles southeast of Hanoi. His eldest son lives in Ho Chi Minh City while his other family members live nearby and still cultivate the land originally worked by Nguyen before he left to fight in the South. Since his wife Vu Thi Gai passed, he reports his life has become very lonely, but since meeting Reed, he reports that he is happy he had the experience of meeting his former enemy and of their subsequent friendship. He says he would not be where he is today had it not been for their original meeting years ago.

Vu Thi Gai, Nghia's wife who told her husband that both he and his little book she gave him would return to her, and amazingly—they both did. She passed in 2008.

Paul Reed raised his son Silas as a single father, and he's now the grandfather of two handsome boys, ages five and six. Reed says he learned the value of writing and speaking and how it can be very cathartic in relieving oneself of personal or emotional pain and passed his discovery along to other 173rd Airborne Brigade combat veterans. He and Ralph Gillum developed a venue allowing them to tell their experiences during times of combat with the unit. Together they founded a website known as the HerdHistoryProject.com. The site offers those veterans the opportunity to have their place in the unit's history. Reed says his mission in life has become to spread the word of peace, reconciliation, and forgiveness. He remarried and now lives in the suburbs of Dallas.

Steve Smith. Smith is a Marine Corps veteran who served two tours of duty in Vietnam. He graduated from Oregon State University and became a television news cameraman for the King Broadcasting Company. He worked as an assignment editor, a newscast producer, and a special projects producer. He left television news in 1979 to start his own production company, making documentaries. Steve has created over two hundred documentaries for home and networks and is a four-time Emmy nominee and sixteen-time Telly Award winner, working in various roles such as cameraman, producer, writer, and editor.

Phil Sturholm, part of Smith's original film crew filming over fifty hours capturing Nghia's and Reed's friendship. Sturholm was an Army veteran. He graduated from Oregon State University and became a television news cameraman for the King Broadcasting Company. He had an amazing career and received more than thirty Emmy Awards. He was inducted into the prestigious Silver Circle, an honor reserved for the best of the best. As a chief photographer, he led a newsroom that received the National Press Photographer's Association, News Station of the Year award three times. He also worked for *Evening Magazine* as a producer-cameraman and the executive producer of two different news organizations. Phil passed in 2016.

The Diary. Ironically, the cherished little book that accomplished so much in the lives of many wound up getting lost. Nguyen Van Nghia regretfully reported that he lost it on a train trip in North Vietnam. "It served its purpose. It did the work it was supposed to do and then moved on," Reed mused philosophically. He couldn't help but think upon hearing of its loss that the power of the little book lives on somewhere else.

ABOUT THE AUTHOR

After trucking nearly twenty years, Reed contributed a short story to a book that was being compiled, *Vietnam: Our Story, One on One*. Gary Gullickson, a fellow U.S. Marine, Vietnam veteran and friend, asked various acquaintances to write a story for his book, which sounded interesting, so Reed said yes. The chapter would be his first experience in writing. Later he co-authored a book with Ted Schwarz titled *Kontum Diary: Captured Writings Bring Peace to a Vietnam Veteran*. While writing the book, Steve Smith of Echo Productions invited him to be an Associate Producer of two PBS documentary films, which he and Nguyen Van Nghia were to be the subject matter. Reed accepted. The films became known as *Kontum Diary*, garnering an Emmy award, among others, then its sequel *Kontum Diary: The Journey Home*.

While Mr. Nguyen Van Nghia was in the United States for medical care, Reed's and Nguyen Van Nghia's reconciliation and forgiveness story was featured in *People* magazine's "Men at Peace." Near that time, both men were invited to appear on the *Good Morning Texas* show for a thirty-minute airtime interview. Shortly after escorting Nghia back to Vietnam, Reed was invited to be a guest of Bryant Gumbel on the *Today* show. Several months later, CBS's *48 Hours* produced a program for broadcast known as *The Fight to Forgive* hosted by Peter Van Zant and Dan Rather.

Reed's army honors include the Bronze Star, Purple Heart, Air Medal, Good Conduct Medal, the Combat Infantryman's Badge, and, among others, a Jumpmaster's qualification. He was honorably discharged before attending junior college in Fort Worth, Texas, selling Harley Davidson motorcycles in Fort Worth, Texas, buying and operating a feed store also in Fort Worth, and driving Interstate trucks throughout the Pacific Northwest and middle to western Canada. His most cherished civilian tributes are the Hero of Forgiveness award from the Worldwide Forgiveness Alliance (forgivenessday.org) headquartered in San Francisco and The Legion of Honor Award from the Chapel of Four Chaplains (fourchaplains.org) based in Philadelphia in recognition of his service to all people without regard to nationality or faith. More recently, he was presented with the Veterans Commendation Award by former Vietnam prisoner of war and United States Congressman Sam Johnson for exceptional service to the country and community, both past and present.

Reed has made many trips to Thai Binh Province in northern Vietnam to visit Nghia and his family. During some of his trips, several veteran friends traveled along. Similarly, they received much healing and now view their old enemy as friends. Consequently, a new non-profit veteran's organization was founded.

The sole mission of Valor Veterans is to provide a path for combat warriors to find peace with the emotional wounds of war by decompressing and reconnecting with themselves and others. Events and programs are specifically designed to reach that goal. Submit your email address via the web address below to receive news and updates regarding the organization's ongoing efforts of assisting veterans. Those interested in supporting this ongoing mission may donate by going to valorveterans.org.

CPSIA information can be obtained
at www.ICGtesting.com
Printed in the USA
LVHW070556230721
693431LV00017B/373

9 781637 690284